More Praise for *The Honor Code*

"A compelling read and represents a refreshingly concrete solution to the question of how to alter deeply objectionable, deeply intractable human practices."　　　*—Publishers Weekly*

"[Appiah's] detailed, concretely researched accounts make this book a true page-turner. . . . These accounts of serious changes in moral standards will immensely interest readers concerned with the ethics of social change. . . . Highly recommended."

　　　　　　—American Library Association

"An enlightening and bold book . . . has offered the foundation for a creative and provocative solution to one of the world's more notorious evils."　　　*—The Daily Beast*

"A thought-provoking, troubling book. . . . It urgently needs to be read."　　　*—Library Journal*

"An eminently readable philosophical discussion of morality based on historical examples. . . . Readers who normally shy away from philosophical subjects will be pleasantly surprised."

　　　　　　—Kirkus Reviews

"What causes moral progress? In this brilliant book, Kwame Anthony Appiah casts light on the role played by honor. This classical concept can be a lodestar in guiding us to a better future. It's an amazing and fascinating insight. This is an indispensable book for both moral philosophers and honorable citizens."

　　　—Walter Isaacson, author of *Einstein: His Life and Universe*

"How stimulating it is to read the remarkable research of a brilliant mind into the concept of honor as the origin of morality as we know it, practiced or not! With fluency of argument and erudition, Appiah charts how history, philosophy, and psychology in action are sustained by patterns of behavior and feeling. This book is essential for us—inescapable in its urgent relevance to the embattled human morality we live within our codes of the present."   —Nadine Gordimer, author of *Telling Times*

"Appiah lays out a concept that is not only compelling in its own right but also suggests a connection that may in time help to collate biological and cultural exploration of human morality."
          —Edward O. Wilson, author of *Sociobiology*

"Kwame Anthony Appiah's recent work has explored a scandalously neglected area of ethical theory: what motivates us to do the right thing? This book offers an important contribution to this area, by looking at honor codes—another neglected zone. . . . A deeply insightful exposition of the dangers, the potential, and the (perhaps) ineradicable role of the human sense of honor."
          —Charles Taylor, author of *A Secular Age*

The Honor Code

Also by Kwame Anthony Appiah

Africana: The Encyclopedia of the African and African-American Experience (coedited with Henry Louis Gates Jr.)

Cosmopolitanism: Ethics in a World of Strangers

Experiments in Ethics

In My Father's House: Africa in the Philosophy of Culture

The Ethics of Identity

Thinking It Through: An Introduction to Contemporary Philosophy

The Honor Code

HOW MORAL REVOLUTIONS HAPPEN

Kwame Anthony Appiah

W. W. NORTON & COMPANY

New York   London

For information about permission to reproduce selections from
this book, write to Permissions, W. W. Norton & Company, Inc.,
500 Fifth Avenue, New York, NY 10110

For information about special discounts for bulk purchases, please contact
W. W. Norton Special Sales at specialsales@wwnorton.com or 800-233-4830

Manufacturing by Courier Westford
Book design by Helene Berinsky
Production manager: Devon Zahn

Library of Congress Cataloging-in-Publication Data

Appiah, Anthony.
The honor code : how moral revolutions happen /
Kwame Anthony Appiah. — 1st ed.
p. cm.
Includes bibliographical references and index.
ISBN 978-0-393-07162-7 (hardcover)
1. Social change—History. 2. Social change—Moral and ethical aspects.
3. Honor—Social aspects—History. 4. Social ethics. I. Title.
HM836.A67 2010
303.48'409—dc22
2010019086

ISBN 978-0-393-34052-5 pbk.

W. W. Norton & Company, Inc.
500 Fifth Avenue, New York, N.Y. 10110
www.wwnorton.com

W. W. Norton & Company Ltd.
Castle House, 75/76 Wells Street, London W1T 3QT

1 2 3 4 5 6 7 8 9 0

magistris meis
et vivis et mortuis

It would be a sort of irreligion, and scarcely less than a libel on human nature, to believe that there is any established and reputable profession or employment, in which a man may not continue to act with honesty and honor; and doubtless there is likewise none which may not at times present temptations to the contrary.

— Samuel Taylor Coleridge, *Biographia Literaria* (1817)

CONTENTS

PREFACE

This book began with a simple question: What can we learn about morality by exploring moral revolutions? I was led to ask it because historians and philosophers have discovered a great deal about science through the careful study of scientific revolutions. Thomas Kuhn and Paul Feyerabend, for example, drew fascinating conclusions from explorations of the seventeenth-century Scientific Revolution—which gave us Galileo, Copernicus, and Newton—and of the more recent revolution that brought us the astonishing theories of quantum physics.

The growth of scientific knowledge has obviously spurred a massive explosion in technology. But the driving spirit of science is not to change the world but to understand it. Morality, on the other hand, as Immanuel Kant insisted, is ultimately practical: though it matters morally what we think and feel, morality is, at its heart, about what we do. So, since a revolution is a large change in a short time, a moral revolution has to involve a rapid transformation in moral *behavior*, not just in moral sentiments. Nevertheless, at the end of the moral revolution, as at the end of a scientific revolution, things look new. Looking back, even over a single generation, people ask, "What were we thinking? How did we do *that* for all those years?"

And so I began to examine a number of moral revolutions, looking to see what could be learned from them. I noticed almost immediately that the disparate cases I looked at—the collapse of the duel, the abandonment of footbinding, the end of Atlantic slavery—had some unexpected features in common. One was that arguments against each of these practices were well known and clearly made a good deal before they came to an end. Not only were the arguments already there, they were made in terms that we—in other cultures or other times—can recognize and understand. Whatever happened when these immoral practices ceased, it wasn't, so it seemed to me, that people were bowled over by new moral arguments. Dueling was always murderous and irrational; footbinding was always painfully crippling; slavery was always an assault on the humanity of the slave.

This was a surprise about what had not happened. The second—and, for me, much more surprising—observation was about what *had*: in each of these transitions, something that was naturally called "honor" played a central role. This led to the inquiry whose results are gathered in this book. It is, of course, hardly astounding that dueling had to do with honor; nor even that the end of dueling came with new ideas about honor. But it *is* striking, to my mind, that ideas about national honor and the honor of workingmen far removed from the plantations of the New World figured so largely in the ending of footbinding and of modern slavery, respectively.

It turned out that these issues also connected pretty immediately with questions about the role of our social identities—as men and women, gay and straight, Americans and Ghanaians, Christians, Muslims, and Jews—in shaping our sentiments and our choices. In an earlier book, I had explored some of the ways in which identifications with families, ethnic groups, religions, and nations could bind us to others in pride and shame. So I was perhaps especially prepared to see the connections between honor and identity that are at the heart of the moral revolutions I'll be discussing.

This seems to me a connection well worth noticing. Identity connects these moral revolutions with an aspect of our human psychology that was widely neglected by moral philosophers working in English for too long, though it has come into sharper focus in recent moral and political philosophy: and that is our deep and persistent concern with status and respect, our human need for what Georg Wilhelm Friedrich Hegel called *Anerkennung*—recognition. We human beings need others to respond appropriately to who we are and to what we do. We need others to recognize us as conscious beings and to acknowledge that we recognize them. When you glance at another person on the street and your eyes meet in mutual acknowledgment, both of you are expressing a fundamental human need, and both of you are responding— instantaneously and without effort—to that need you identify in each other. Hegel's most famous discussion of the struggle for recognition comes in the exploration of the relationship of master and slave in the *Phenomenology of Spirit*. He would not, I think, have been surprised that something of the energy of the movements to abolish slavery came from a search for recognition.

So my inquiry led me somewhere a little unexpected: I want now to claim a crucial place for honor in our thinking about what it is to live a successful human life. Aristotle thought that the best life was one in which you achieved something he called *eudaimonia*, and he called the study of *eudaimonia* "ethics." I think of this book as a contribution to ethics in Aristotle's sense, which is the sense in which I aim to use the word myself.

Eudaimonia has been misleadingly translated as "happiness," but what Aristotle meant is better captured by saying that to have *eudaimonia* is to flourish; and I would gloss flourishing as "living well," so long as you don't think that the only thing to living well is being good to others. The values that guide us in deciding what we owe to others are a subset of the many values that guide our lives, and I think it is reasonable to call that special kind of value moral value. Dueling, footbinding, and slavery are obviously, in this sense, moral issues. (Slaves and footbound women and dead duelists are denied their due.)

Clearly, morality, in this sense, is an important dimension of ethics: doing what I should for others is part of living well, and one of the distinctive features of the last few centuries has been a growing appreciation of the obligations each of us has to other people. But there is much more to a good life than being morally good; and it is a besetting temptation of philosophy to scant the great multiplicity of the things that make human lives go well. A good life usually includes relationships with family and friends, which are governed not just by what we owe to others but also by what we freely give them out of love. Most of us also have our lives made better by social activity. We participate in a church or a temple; we play or watch sports together; we get involved in local and national politics. And we profit, too, from exposure to some of the many things that are valuable in human experience, including

music, literature, film, and the visual arts, as well as from participation in the sorts of projects that we choose for ourselves, such as
learning to cook well, or making a garden, or studying the history
of our families. There are many kinds of human good.

One way to begin to grasp why honor matters to ethics is to
recognize the connections between honor and respect; for respect
and self-respect are clearly central human goods, too, things that
add to *eudaimonia*, helping us to live well.

I have spent a good deal of my scholarly life trying to get my
fellow philosophers to recognize both the theoretical and the
practical importance of things that they may have taken too little
notice of: race and ethnicity, gender and sexuality, nationality and
religion . . . all of the rich social identities with which we make our
lives. Honor, it turns out, is another crucial topic modern moral
philosophy has neglected. And one reason why it is crucial is that
like our social identities, it connects our lives together. Attending
to honor, too, like noticing the importance of our social identities,
can help us both to treat others as we should and to make the best
of our own lives. Philosophers once knew this—read Montesquieu
or Adam Smith or, for that matter, Aristotle. But, though "respect"
and "self-respect" are in pretty good odor in contemporary philosophy, the related but distinct concept of "honor" seems to have
been largely forgotten. It is time, I suggest, to restore honor to
philosophy.

The historical episodes I explore in this book exemplify—and
thus allow us to explore—different features of the way honor works
across space and time. Each of them allows us to add elements to
the picture. By following a journey from Britain to China, then
back again to the Atlantic world, we shall be able to acquire a

deepening grasp of honor's many dimensions. These are not three separate local stories but strands of one human story, a story that matters as much for people in Singapore or Mumbai or Rio de Janeiro as for those in Los Angeles or Cape Town or Berlin. And in every one of those places, I am sure, though there are local variations on honor's themes, we could find episodes that would teach the same core lessons.

My aim, though, is not just to understand other people, other times, and other places but also to illuminate our lives now. In particular, I want to use the lessons we can draw from the past to address one of the most challenging problems that honor poses in the contemporary world: the murder of women and girls in the name of honor. When we travel to Pakistan in chapter 4, we will be ready both to understand and to confront one of the dark sides of honor; and, as with the historical cases, the lessons we learn from one place apply elsewhere. I focus on Pakistan, but it is important to be clear from the start that it is far from being the only place where honor murder occurs today.

Honor killing is not the only way honor is at work today, and my aim in the final chapter is to suggest ways in which making sense of honor can help us grapple with other contemporary problems. "What were they thinking?" we ask about our ancestors, but we know that, a century hence, our descendents will ask the same thing about us. Who knows what will strike them as strangest? The United States incarcerates 1 percent of its population and subjects many thousands of inmates to years of solitary confinement. In Saudi Arabia, women are forbidden to drive. There are countries today in which homosexuality is punishable by life in prison or by death. Then there's the sequestered reality of factory farming, in which hundreds of millions of mammals, and billions of birds, live a squalid, brief existence. Or the toleration of extreme poverty, inside and outside the developed world. One day, people will find themselves thinking not just that an old practice was wrong and a new one right but that there was something shameful in the old ways. In the course of the transition, many will change what they do because they are shamed out of an old way of doing things. So it is perhaps not too much to hope that if we can find the proper place for honor now, we can make the world better. This book aims to explain honor in order to help us recognize its continuing importance for every one of us.

When I was a boy, the Irish singer Val Doonican had a hit called "Walk Tall," in which he sang about what his mama told him when he was "about knee-high." "Walk tall," she said; she also urged him to "look the world right in the eye." Though I was only a little more than knee-high myself, I recall how this maternal admonition called to me (even though the character in the song was speaking from a prison cell where failure to respect his mama's advice had led him). Val Doonican had a lovely voice and his hit had a great tune; but the reason that it has stuck with me over more than forty years is surely its simple articulation of an ideal of honor. The psychology of honor is deeply connected with walking tall and looking the world in the eye. Val's mama also told him he should hold his "head up high"; and when able-bodied people with a sense of honor remember they are entitled to respect, they literally walk with their heads held high. We can see their self-respect; and they can feel it in the inflation of their chests and the straightening of their spines.

Humiliation, on the other hand, curves the spine, lowers the eyes. In Asante-Twi, my father's language, when someone does something dishonorable, we say, "His face has fallen"; and, indeed, shame's face is the face of a person with eyes cast down. If we have a word for honor in Twi it is *animuonyam*, a word containing the root *nim*, which means "face." Everyone knows that the Chinese speak of "losing face"; but in French and in German, as in English, one can lose and save face, too. East Asia, Western Europe, and West Africa: three very different zones. That suggests that human beings everywhere might have these basic propensities.

What you do deliberately with your face—whether you present it boldly or hide it away—is not the only thing that matters. We blush involuntarily with shame; and tears well up in our eyes when we feel intensely, especially when we experience such moral emotions as indignation and pride. It is through the face above all else that we see what others are feeling, and so honor's preoccupation with the face might seem to suggest that honor engages our feelings only when we are on view. But that, of course, would be a mistake. Shame is something you can experience all on your own.

Back in the seventeenth century, René Descartes wrote that he was "forced to admit that I blush with shame to think that in the past I have praised this author. . . ."[1] We imagine him sitting in his study, reflecting on his past praise and realizing that he has displayed terrible judgment; the sort of misjudgment that means that he is no longer worthy of complete intellectual respect. The blood rushes to his face. To care for your honor is to want to be worthy of respect. If you realize you have done something that makes you unworthy, you feel shame whether or not anyone is watching.

By the end of the book, I will have introduced you to what you might call a "theory of honor." But I think that the best way to get there is to come upon the crucial elements of the way honor works by seeing it in action in the lives of individuals and communities. At the start of the final chapter, I will assemble all the elements of the theory that we have discovered together. That is, I think, the right place for the full statement. Because theories are not much use without the arguments for them; and until you know why I make certain claims, you won't really be able to make much sense of them . . . or be able to decide whether I am right.

Now I know that many contemporary people dislike talk of "honor" and think that we would be better off without it. (That's the sort of thing you learn when you spend a few years where the answer to "What are you up to?" is "Writing a book about honor.") But whether you are for or against honor, I am sure you recognize feelings like Descartes' shame and Val Doonican's pride. It is a central fact about human beings that our societies create codes that are sustained by such patterns of behavior and of feeling; the heart of the psychology of honor—the giving and receiving of respect—is already in you as it is in every normal human being, however enlightened and advanced. That is one reason why I think we need to reckon with honor. It draws on fundamental tendencies in human social psychology. And it is surely better to understand our nature and manage it than to announce that we would rather we were different . . . or, worse, pretend we don't have a nature at all. We may think we have finished with honor, but honor isn't finished with us.

—Kwame Anthony Appiah
Princeton, New Jersey

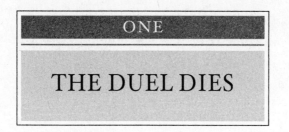

ONE

THE DUEL DIES

. . . equality is indispensable.

—Rule XIV of *The Irish Practice of*
Duelling and the Point of Honour

AN AWKWARD ENCOUNTER

A little before eight on the morning of March 21, 1829, the Duke of Wellington, England's prime minister, arrived on horseback at a crossroads south of the Thames, about half a mile beyond Battersea Bridge. Not long after, his cabinet colleague, Sir Henry Hardinge, the secretary of war, rode up to join him, followed, after another small interval, by the duke's doctor, in a coach.

Once the three men had greeted one another, the doctor walked past a small farmhouse into a large open area called Battersea Fields with a pair of pistols concealed under his greatcoat, and placed the weapons out of sight behind a hedge. Battersea Fields was well known as a site where gentlemen met to fight duels, and anyone who had witnessed this sequence of arrivals would have known what was going on. Almost every Londoner would have recognized the duke, whose face, with the great Roman nose and high forehead, had been famous since his first victories over Napoleon's armies in Spain, twenty years earlier. Any onlookers would have been curious, as a result, to see who would arrive next.

After all, once a gentleman, his second, and his doctor had appeared, you could anticipate the arrival of an opponent with *his* second. That the upright duke, who was the epitome of honor, a model of service to king and country, was preparing to fight a duel would naturally raise the question who could have impugned his honor.

And that question was soon answered when the three men

were joined by the Earl of Winchilsea and his second, the Earl of Falmouth. Lord Winchilsea's baptismal name was George William Finch-Hatton. (His grandson, Denys Finch-Hatton, was the handsome English aristocrat played by Robert Redford in the film *Out of Africa*.) Finch-Hatton was a good deal less famous than the duke, such notoriety as he had being due to his active opposition over the last year or two to the movement to lift some of the legal burdens on Catholics in Britain (burdens that had been in place, in one form or another, since the Reformation). An inspiring orator, he had spoken out often in and out of Parliament on the need to protect the faith and traditions of his fathers. He was a leader among those Englishmen who continued to believe fervently that you could not be loyal both to Britain and, as they saw it, to the Pope in Rome. Winchilsea was tall, black-haired, and powerfully built. He was in his late thirties, more than twenty years younger than the duke. He must have cut an imposing figure as he rode in with Falmouth, who was, like him, a former military officer.

The Duke of Wellington stood aloof while the two seconds, Falmouth and Hardinge, engaged in a heated exchange. Then the doctor loaded the pistols he had hidden behind the hedge—this was strictly speaking Hardinge's job, but Hardinge had lost his left hand in the Napoleonic wars—while Lord Falmouth loaded one of the two pistols that he had brought with him. Hardinge picked a spot for the duke, marched twelve paces, and instructed Lord Winchilsea to take up his position. Wellington objected to the first positioning. "Damn it," he said. "Don't stick him up so near the ditch. If I hit him, he will tumble in."[1]

Finally, once their places were set, Hardinge gave the duke a pistol, Falmouth took one to Winchilsea, and Hardinge stepped back and, after a few more formalities, said firmly: "Gentlemen, are you ready? Fire." The duke raised his pistol and, following a brief pause apparently prompted by the fact that the earl had made no preparations, he discharged it. Winchilsea was unharmed. The earl then raised his pistol very deliberately over his head and fired into the air.

Wellington's doctor reported later a version of the exchange between the two seconds that followed:

> The Duke remained still on his place, but Lord Falmouth and Lord Winchilsea came immediately forward towards Sir Henry Hardinge, and Lord Falmouth, addressing him, said, "Lord Winchilsea, having received the Duke's fire, is placed under different circumstances from those in which he stood before, and now feels himself at liberty to give the Duke the reparation he desires."

Falmouth was following the convention that all communications should take place through the seconds, and Sir Henry, as the duke's second, had the duty of replying. And so, after a tense few seconds pause, Hardinge said:

> "The Duke expects an ample apology, and a complete and full acknowledgement of his error in having published the accusation against him which he has done." To which Lord Falmouth answered, "I mean an apology in the most extensive or in every sense of the word"; and he then took from his pocket a written paper containing what he called an admission from Lord Winchilsea that he was wrong. . . .[2]

After further lively discussion and an amendment proposed by the doctor, all parties agreed upon a slightly edited version of the apology that Falmouth had prepared.

The duke approached and bowed to the two earls, and Falmouth, who had clearly been a reluctant participant in the proceedings, explained that he had always thought Winchilsea was completely in the wrong. Hardinge now made it plain that *he* thought that if Falmouth felt this way, he shouldn't have acted as Winchilsea's second; and when Falmouth made a further attempt to explain himself, this time to the duke, Wellington interrupted him. "My Lord Falmouth," he said, "I have nothing to do with these matters." Then he raised two fingers to the brim of his hat, said, "Good morning, my Lord Winchilsea, good morning, my Lord Falmouth," and got back on his horse.

In exploring this infamous passage of arms and the responses to it, we can come to understand the changing culture of honor in Britain in the first half of the nineteenth century. The death of the duel in Britain—the disappearance of a practice that had defined the lives of gentlemen for some three centuries—is the first of the moral revolutions I want to explore. And Wellington and Winchilsea's encounter on Battersea Fields allows us to witness some of the pressures that brought it to an end.

CONSTITUTIONAL CHALLENGES

The duel had its origins in Winchilsea's vociferous opposition to a bill that Wellington had been shepherding through the House of Lords: the Catholic Relief Act, which would permit Catholics to sit in the British Parliament for the first time in over a hundred and fifty years. A year earlier, in June 1828, Daniel O'Connell, the Irish patriot and founder of the Catholic Association, which aimed to improve the situation of Catholics in Ireland, had been elected to the British Parliament. O'Connell and his policies were enormously popular in Ireland, as the election showed, and his presence in London would have allowed their views expression in the legislature. But because he was a Catholic, he could not be seated in the House of Commons . . . unless he was willing to swear an oath that "the invocation or adoration of the Virgin Mary or any other Saint, and the Sacrifice of the Mass, as they are now used in the Church of Rome, are superstitious and idolatrous. . . ." Obviously, no self-respecting Catholic could swear to that. Equally obviously, that was exactly why the oath was required. And this exclusion from Parliament reflected the many other exclusions Catholic Irishmen and women faced in their own country. Feelings in Ireland ran high about the issue and there was talk, in some quarters, of civil war.

Like most Tories, including Sir Robert Peel, who steered the bill through the House of Commons, Wellington had once opposed Catholic emancipation, and neither statesman had changed his mind casually. The duke, who was born in Ireland and had been Chief Secretary for Ireland as a young politician, was particularly well placed to appreciate the delicacy of the situation in that troubled island. He had changed his position on Catholic emancipation because, as he observed in his speech on the second reading of the bill in the House of Lords—a speech that many regarded as one of the best of his parliamentary career—Ireland seemed to be in a state "bordering on civil war." And, the king's first minister added, to cheers in that august chamber, "I must say this—that if I could avoid, by any sacrifice whatever, even one month of civil war in the country to which I am attached, I would sacrifice my life in order to do it."[3]

But George William Finch-Hatton, tenth Earl of Winchilsea, was pleased to assume the worst, and he often avowed, as the bill's final passage drew near, that the Duke of Wellington was plotting an assault on the Protestant constitution. In a broadside in February 1829, Winchilsea had urged his "BROTHER PROTESTANTS! . . . boldly to stand forward in Defense of our Protestant Constitution and Religion. . . ." Because the "great body of your degenerate Senators are prepared to sacrifice, at the shrine of Treason and Rebellion, that Constitution for which our Ancestors so nobly fought and died," he called upon his countrymen to petition King and Parliament. He subscribed himself modestly the "humble and devoted servant" of his Protestant brethren, signing the flyer, not so humbly perhaps, "Winchilsea and Nottingham," since he happened to be the fifth Earl of Nottingham as well.

In a letter to the newspaper, the *Standard*, published on March 16, about a week before the bill finally passed, Winchilsea made a more specific attack upon the Duke of Wellington. He alleged that the king's first minister had dissembled in offering his financial support for the creation of King's College London as an Anglican institution to counterbalance the recent secular foundation of London University. The duke's involvement in this ostentatiously Protestant project was a "blind," Winchilsea claimed, that would allow him, "under the cloak of some outward show of zeal for the Protestant religion," to "carry on his insidious designs for the infringement of our liberties, and the introduction of Popery into every department of the State."[4]

No one could doubt that Winchilsea felt strongly about the English Church. Charles Greville—who served as clerk to the Privy Council, the body that included all the monarch's senior political advisers, from 1821 to 1859—described him as "a peer of no personal importance, but a stalwart upholder of Church and State."[5] Still, accusing the hero of the wars against Napoleon, the "Saviour of Europe" and the victor of Waterloo, of dissembling about his true faith and betraying the Constitution was surely—as the gentlemen in the London clubs among whom the accusation circulated might have put it—going too far.

Stung, as it seemed, by Winchilsea's published charge, Wellington insisted that the earl apologize . . . which the latter, after a hurried exchange of notes, declined to do. And so, on March 20, the duke sent him a scornful message in which he asked: "Is the King's Minister to submit to be insulted by any gentleman who thinks proper to attribute to him disgraceful or criminal motives for his conduct as an individual?" And he answered himself immediately: "I cannot doubt of the decision which I ought to make on this question. Your lordship alone is responsible for the consequences." He therefore insisted that Winchilsea grant him "that satisfaction which a gentleman has a right to require and which a gentleman never refuses to give."[6] The next morning, the duke and the earl met with their seconds on Battersea Fields.

A few weeks later, the Catholic Relief Act gained George IV's royal assent and, with it, the force of law. It was rumored that the anti-Catholic king had wept as he signed the bill, compelled to do so by Wellington's threat to resign.

WHAT WAS HE THINKING?

Such were the circumstances that gave rise to Wellington's challenge. But now consider this. The duke was not an enthusiast for dueling. Indeed, unlike many military officers of his day, and despite an immensely distinguished military career, he had never dueled previously and he never did so again. While he was a field commander in the Napoleonic wars, he apparently believed that British military honor would be diminished if dueling were totally suppressed in the army. But in 1843, fourteen years after the infamous duel while he was still commander in chief, the Articles of War were amended to institute serious penalties for dueling in all branches of the armed forces, after lobbying by many prominent figures, including Queen Victoria's beloved husband, Prince Albert. In later life the duke was a prominent member of the Anti-Duelling Association.

What's more, dueling was unlawful. As Sir William Blackstone had written in the 1760s, in his *Commentaries on the Laws of England,* the common law of England "justly fixed the crime and punishment of murder" upon duelers and their seconds, who "wanton with their own lives and those of their fellow creatures."[7] Canon law and Christian moral teaching opposed the duel, too.

Then there were the *political* implications. Had he been killed, the country and the king would have lost a prime minister in the midst of a constitutional crisis in an illegal affair that was *about* the issues at stake in that crisis. Few things could have been more destabilizing in an already unsettled realm. Had he killed Winchilsea, on the other hand, the duke would have had to be tried before the House of Lords for murder. (As Lord Cardigan was to be tried in 1841 for wounding a Captain Tuckett in a duel: their lordships acquitted.)[8] At a minimum, he would surely have had to resign from the cabinet, just as two other Anglo-Irish politicians, Canning and Castlereagh, had had to resign as foreign secretary and secretary of war respectively after their own duel two decades earlier. In either case, there is reason to doubt that the House of Lords would have passed the Catholic Relief Act.

Had there been a trial, the Lords would have faced a difficult choice. The French Revolution and the execution of Louis XVI and his queen in 1793 had raised the banner of republicanism in Europe. The Jacobin Club—the leading radical organization of the Revolution—spread new ideas about liberty and equality through France, which quickly gained adherents in England as well. At the turn of the nineteenth century, British governments took measures regularly to confront the threat of Jacobinism, fearing a rising tide of hostility not just to the monarchy but to the aristocracy and, indeed, to all inherited privilege.

After Wellington defeated Napoleon at Waterloo, there was a period of high unemployment, exacerbated by the so-called Corn Laws, which aimed at keeping out cheap grain. These laws protected the economic interests of the farmers who grew wheat and similar crops in the United Kingdom, but raised the cost of food for the British poor. The flagrant insensitivity of the ruling classes to the sufferings of the worst-off added impetus to radical demands. In 1819, more than 50,000 men and women gathered at St. Peter's Field in Manchester to press for parliamentary reform. When they refused a magistrate's order to disperse, members of the military class that Wellington represented cut down ordinary men and women in the streets, killing a dozen men and three women, half a dozen of them sabered before they were trampled to death. The massacre was called "Peterloo," a none too subtle reference to the slaughter at Wellington's greatest victory.

By 1829, then, as the Catholic Relief Act was being debated, many in Parliament and the country were agitating for more substantial reforms and they were being resisted by a highly unrepresentative Parliament, dominated by an unelected aristocracy. It was not a good moment for the authorities to look mildly on a serious breach of the peace by an aristocrat while they were dealing with the lower orders with such violent resolve. And, in the unlikely event that his peers declined to excuse him, they would have imposed that unpopular task on the king, since actually executing Wellington was out of the question.

In sum, dueling was contrary to Wellington's own inclinations, to civil law and to Christian teaching, and, so it might seem, to political prudence. So what was the first minister of a king who was also head of the Church of England doing out there in Battersea at eight o'clock that brisk spring morning? What on earth was he thinking? Well, as anyone in the small knot of curious bystanders could have told you, Arthur Wellesley, Knight of the Bath, Baron Douro of Wellington, Viscount Wellington of Talavera and of Wellington, Earl of Wellington, Marquess of Wellington and of Douro, and Duke of Wellington (to supply his full battery of titles) was defending his honor as a gentleman.

THE FORMS OF RESPECT

According to the codes that governed his society and his class, Wellington had the right as a gentleman to be treated with respect by other gentlemen, a prerogative flagrantly violated by Winchilsea's public accusation. At the heart of honor, then, is this simple idea: Having honor means being entitled to respect.

But what do we mean by respect? The philosopher Stephen Darwall has recently distinguished two fundamentally different ways in which we may respect a person. One, which he calls "appraisal respect," involves judging a person positively according to a standard. And doing well by a standard essentially means doing better than most others. It is in this sense that we respect Rafael Nadal for his tennis skills or Meryl Streep for her acting. (I shall often use the word "esteem" for this kind of respect.) Wellington was hardly indifferent to such respect. As a soldier he had lived up to the highest standards of military achievement. The honor that came to him as a result was competitive: he got it by doing better than other people. Most of his many titles were given him out of respect for those achievements.

But there is another kind of respect, "recognition respect," that involves (to put it rather abstractly) treating people in ways that give appropriate weight to some fact about them. When we respect powerful people—a judge in court, say, or a police officer when we're out driving—we treat them warily because they have the capacity to compel us to do things. Our respect *recognizes* the fact of that power. But we can also respect a sensitive person, by speaking to him gently, or a disabled person, by assisting her when she asks for help. Respecting people in this sense, in other words, doesn't require you to rate them especially highly.

Because there are so many kinds of facts about people we can recognize and respond to, recognition respect for people can have a great variety of emotional tones and can come along with attitudes both positive and negative. When the Roman emperor Caligula said, "*Oderint dum metuant*—Let them hate so long as they fear," he was expressing his depraved delight in getting one sort of respect; but it wasn't the sort of positive respect that goes with honor.

As a result, the sort of recognition respect that is important for honor involves more than just "giving appropriate weight to some fact about " a person. It also requires, especially as we conceive it today, a positive attitude of a certain sort. I think, in fact, that the relevant attitude is the very one we display when we esteem people highly. So, from now on, when I talk about recognition respect, I mean the kind that involves a positive regard for the person in virtue of the fact that it recognizes. Though this regard is found in esteem as well, it remains important, as we shall see, to distinguish the different bases of the judgments associated with these different sorts of respect.

These two kinds of respect—esteem and positive recognition respect—correspond to two kind of honor. There is competitive honor, which comes in degrees; but there is also what we could call "peer honor," which governs relations among equals. (This is a conceptual distinction; I don't say that these two kinds of honor are always tidily compartmentalized in actual usage.) Peer honor does not come by degrees: either you have it or you do not.

Henry V of England—Shakespeare's Prince Hal—was born to honor, owing to his royal parentage, but he was especially proud of the competitive honor he achieved from his military prowess, as at the battle of Agincourt, where his armies defeated the massed forces of the French king ("for as I am a soldier, / A name that in my thoughts becomes me best," he says in Act III, Sc. iii). A fifteenth-century warrior king not only ruled his realm, he also led his armies. His unearned royal honor was supplemented by the martial honor he earned for himself.

There are frequent evocations of the martial ideal in the literature of chivalry: in the stories, for example, of the knights of King Arthur's Round Table that were staples of the education of upper-class boys in England well into the twentieth century. In the earliest literary version of these tales, the *Morte D'Arthur*—which Sir Thomas Malory probably began in the 1450s as a prisoner in the Tower of London, where Henry V's son and heir, Henry VI, was also incarcerated—Sir Tristram says that he fought "for the love of my uncle king Mark and for the love of the country of Cornwall and to increase my honor."[9] And, indeed, Shakespeare's Henry V says, in the play's most famous speech, at the beginning of the battle at Agincourt:

> *. . . if it be a sin to covet honor*
> *I am the most offending soul alive. (Act IV, Sc. iii)*

Yet competitive honor, of the sort that Sir Tristram and Prince Hal and the Duke of Wellington won in battle, is not the form of honor that the duel served to defend. Wellington treated Winchilsea as a gentleman in challenging him to a duel. In so doing he displayed recognition respect: he treated Winchilsea in a way that gave what was (by the standards of his society) appropriate positive weight to the fact that the earl was a gentleman. In turn, Wellington, though he was clearly entitled to a good deal of appraisal respect as the most successful military commander (and one of the greatest statesmen) of the age, required from Winchilsea only the recognition respect due to any gentleman. It was respect between equals.

The honor of peers is something people of the right station either have, if they keep the codes, or don't have, if they don't. And the respect that gentlemen were supposed to show each other in eighteenth- and early nineteenth-century England was just such respect among equals, grounded not in esteem but in recognition. You owed the same courtesy to one gentleman as you owed to all the others. Provided you were of the right social standing, the respect to which you were entitled as a gentleman, your gentlemanly honor, was no greater whether you were a magnificent military success, like the Duke of Wellington, or an ordinary country squire.

It's important to understand that while honor is an entitlement to respect—and shame comes when you lose that title—a person of honor cares first of all not about being respected but about being *worthy* of respect. Someone who just wants to be respected won't care whether he is really living up to the code; he will just want to be *thought* to be living up to it. He will be managing his reputation, not maintaining his honor. To be honorable you have both to *understand* the honor code and to be *attached* to it: these are the conditions that the anthropologist Frank Henderson Stewart takes to define a *sense of honor*.[10] For the honorable person, honor itself is the thing that matters, not honor's rewards. You feel shame when you have not met the standards of the honor code; and you feel it—remember Descartes—whether or not anyone else knows you have failed.

Shame is the feeling appropriate to one's own dishonorable behavior. (Because of this connection between honor and shame, one way of speaking of those who are especially dishonorable is to say that they are shameless.) The appropriate response from others if you breach the codes is, first, to cease to respect you and, then, actively to treat you with disrespect. The feeling we have for those who have done what is shameful is contempt; and I shall have occasion in this book to make use of the slightly old-fashioned verb "contemn," which means both to regard and to treat contemptuously, just as the verb "honor" means both to regard and to treat with respect.

What you should feel when you are honorable (or act honorably) is a more complicated matter. Pride is shame's opposite, and you might think that it is, therefore, the right response to one's own honorable behavior. But pride seems especially apt when you have done something out of the ordinary; and an honorable person will often think that what he has done is simply what he had to do. If you are truly honorable, you may be no more inclined to be proud of living up to your standards than you are to be pleased with yourself for breathing. Honor can consist in taking the code for granted.

One difficulty for pride, then, is that modesty may be part of an honor code. In chapter 2, I shall discuss another reason why, in the Christian world at least, pride's connection with honor is more complicated than shame's; namely, a tradition of moral hostility to pride (or vanity, as it is called when we are disapproving), an antagonism that goes back to the Stoics.[11] Henry V identifies the problem clearly after he receives the reports of the scale of his victory at Agincourt: "And be it death proclaimed through our host / To boast of this or take the praise from God / Which is His only" (Act IV, Sc. viii).

But other societies—ancient Greece, for example, in the long-ago past, or Asante, where I grew up, even today—have thought that pride and blowing your own horn were the natural accompaniments of honor.[12] There is a saying in my father's language that runs, "A person's honor is like an egg; if he doesn't hold it well, it falls and breaks." Part of making sure you're holding your honor right may be reminding other people that you know your worth. In the *Iliad*, Achilles does nothing to diminish his honor when he says, matter-of-factly:

> *And look, you see how handsome and powerful I am?*
> *The son of a great man, the mother who gave me life*
> *a deathless goddess.*[13]

In Wellington's world, though, this sort of boasting would have been ungentlemanly. You showed your worth in action, not by singing your own praises. For him, the right emotional response to his own honor was not pride but simple self-respect.

I said that the honorable person cares about honor itself, not simply about the social rewards of being considered honorable. Emotions like shame (and pride) are reinforced, it's true, when other people are watching—especially those whose respect matters to me most. Nevertheless, honor requires me to conform to the standard for its own sake, not merely for the sake of reputation and its rewards. And someone who aims at reputation for its own sake is taking a dishonorable short cut.

That is one reason why honesty is so central to honor. (*Honestus* in Latin can mean both "honest" and "honorable.") Accusations of lying were one of the principal causes of duels. The rewards of a good reputation are substantial, and the temptations of getting them without meriting them are therefore substantial, too. Perhaps that is why the penalties in terms of loss of respect—including contempt and eventual ostracism—tend to be severe.

So it's very much to the point that Wellington had been accused by Winchilsea of dishonesty, in trying to distract the public from his support for Catholics by contributing money to a Protestant cause. Had he, in fact, been doing what Winchilsea alleged, it would have been shameful. The code required that, once an allegation of this sort had been made, you had to clear your name: you had to establish that it wasn't true. And the first way to do this was to ask for and receive a public apology. If the apology was denied, the same code required you to challenge your accuser to a duel; and that would show, among other things, that you were willing to risk your life rather than be thought to be guilty of something dishonorable.

The duel displays a slightly awkward amalgam of concern for being shown respect with concern with being worthy of it. What initiates it is a slight of some sort: a display of disrespect. But why, if you are worthy of respect, should the mere fact that someone disrespects you matter? Shouldn't it matter only if their disrespect is justified, as Winchilsea's surely was not? The answer, in Wellington's world, was that the code of the gentleman insists that to be worthy of respect you have to be willing to respond to such slights. A man of honor must be ready to defend his honor—to risk his life, in fact, to ensure that he gets the respect that is his due. Both Wellington and Winchilsea thought that, in dueling, they were defending their honor.

HONOR WORLDS

To be respected is, of course, to be respected *by* somebody. Because of the conceptual connection between honor and being respected, we can always ask whose respect is at stake. Usually, it is not the respect of people in general, it is the respect of some particular social group, which I will call an "honor world": a group of people who acknowledge the same codes. Shakespeare's character Henry V, like his historical model, doesn't care much about the opinions of peasants: he expects their obedience, and no doubt they appraise him highly. But he does expect them both to respect him and to treat him with respect. On the other hand, he won't worry if strangers—faraway Saracens, for example—don't respect him. For one thing, they may not understand the codes by which he lives.

To say that people have honor is to say that they are entitled to respect according to the codes of their honor world. But it's misleading to say that someone has honor when you don't accept those codes yourself. Better, in those circumstances, to say he or she was honored in such and such an honor world. If you and I share the codes, though, we won't need to relativize in this way. Within a common honor world saying, "We honor him" and saying, "He has honor" have the same practical effect.

In taking the measure of Wellington's honor world and its norms, we should notice that, of the ten men who preceded Wellington as prime minister, three—Lord Shelburne, William Pitt the Younger, and Canning—fought duels, as did Charles Fox and the Earl of Bath, each of whom was almost prime minister; and Peel, who eventually followed the Duke to the premiership, had shown himself willing to accept challenges.[14] In the most notorious of these episodes, Canning took to the field in 1809 against Viscount Castlereagh, when they were members of the same government. While this episode led to their resignation from the cabinet, they both went on with political careers of further distinction:

Castlereagh began a decade of service as foreign secretary in 1809, guiding the British alliances that defeated Napoleon; Canning succeeded him as foreign secretary and went on to be prime minister for a few months in 1827.

No one suffered any penalties for his participation in the Wellington-Winchilsea affair. Neither Winchilsea nor Falmouth seems to have been destined for greatness, so perhaps all the evidence we have about them is that there was no prosecution; but Wellington remained prime minister, and Hardinge went on to become Viceroy of India, eventually returning to England in 1852 to succeed the duke as the British army's commander in chief, a position he held during the Crimean War, a few years later.

The duel appealed to the political elites of the new American republic, whose culture was an offshoot of Britain's, as well. A quarter of a century earlier, in July 1804, two of the most prominent politicians in the early American republic, Alexander Hamilton and Aaron Burr, had met in a fatal duel on the Heights of Weehauken in New Jersey; fatal, that is, for Hamilton. Hamilton was one of the authors of the *Federalist Papers* (1788) that continue to define the meaning of the American Constitution; he was also a former secretary of Treasury. Burr was a sitting vice president. And Hamilton's early death—he was not yet fifty—was one of the great scandals of the day. Yet, while Burr was charged with murder in both New Jersey and New York, he was never actually tried, and he saw out his term as vice president, even though many thoroughly disapproved of what he had done.

Burr's freedom from the legal consequences of what was a crime in New Jersey as in Britain would not have surprised anyone in England. It was essentially unheard of, in the century before Wellington and Winchilsea faced each other on Battersea Fields, for a British gentleman who observed the rules of honor to be prosecuted successfully for murdering an opponent in a duel.[15] The standard pattern, if one party was killed, was for the other one to disappear abroad and wait to see if a prosecution was brought. If you were not charged, you could return quietly and go about your business. If you were prosecuted, and you had behaved properly, you would present the facts to a jury of your peers, the judge was quite likely to be sympathetic, and the jury was most likely to acquit you anyway even if he was not. In the unlikely event you were convicted and sentenced to death, connections at court made it likely you would eventually be pardoned. Dueling was one way of literally getting away with murder.

This was not because the authorities were squeamish about executions. In a typical year in the eighteenth century, there were some one hundred executions in England and Wales; in the mid-century, there were more than thirty a year at Tyburn, London's place of public execution, alone. And execution for gentlemen, even members of the House of Lords, was not just a legal possibility: in 1760, a member of the House of Lords, Earl Ferrers, was hanged for murder at Tyburn. No, the reason duelists were not condemned was that the official legal norm conflicted with the social consensus among the British elite.

Indeed, since Wellington's youth, there had almost certainly been an increase in the frequency of dueling, in part because the turn of the nineteenth century was an extended period of warfare. Some half a million Britons had served in the Anglo-French warfare between the execution of Louis XVI in 1793 and the battle of Waterloo.[16] Their officers came back from Europe imbued with the military's culture of honor.

CHANGING CODES

The conduct of Wellington's duel reflected conventions origi-
nating in the early sixteenth century in Italy and codified in
documents such as the Irish Duello or Duel Code "settled at
Clonmel Summer Assizes, 1777, by the gentlemen delegates
of Tipperary, Galway, Mayo, Sligo and Roscommon, and pre-
scribed for general adoption throughout Ireland"—also known
as the "twenty-six commandments."[17] Wellington's challenge,
delivered by his second, Sir Henry Hardinge, a veteran of the
military campaigns in Portugal and Spain that had made Wellington a national hero, required only the mention of a gentleman's demand for satisfaction in order to be understood.
Hardinge had provided a coach to bring Wellington's doctor,
Dr. John Robert Hume, but had not told him on whose behalf
he was being summoned. (This was conventional; because the
duel was illegal, telling him could have opened him up to prosecution as an accessory if things had gone badly.) As a result,
when the good doctor arrived, he was astonished, as he told
the Duchess of Wellington later, to find his patient preparing
to shoot and be shot at. Wellington, laughing, said to Hume:
"Well, I dare say you little expected it was I who wanted you
to be here." And the doctor replied, "Indeed, my Lord, you are
certainly the last person I should have expected here."[18]

There is some dispute as to the proper interpretation of what
happened after Hardinge shouted: "Gentlemen, are you ready?
Fire." Wellington fired first, as we saw, and, according to some
accounts, fired wide deliberately. But it would have been hard to
tell if he was making a good faith effort to shoot the earl, since

dueling pistols were not very reliable and, in any case, though he was a great general, he was apparently not much of a shot.

The correspondence of English ladies of the era abounds in surprisingly sympathetic stories of His Grace's accidents in the chase. Lady Palmerston wrote from Middleton, home of the Earl and Countess of Jersey, on January 16, 1823: "The Duke has been unlucky at Wherstead; he peppered Lord Granville's face with nine shots, fortunately he miss'd his eyes, but it has given him a great deal of pain. . . ."[19] (You might have thought that it was Lord Granville who had been unlucky.) And Frances, Lady Shelley, recounts a day when, after wounding a dog and hitting a game-keeper's gaiters, Wellington ended a chapter of accidents by shooting an old woman who was unwise enough to do her washing by an open window. "I'm wounded, Milady," the woman screamed. "My good woman," Lady Shelley replied, "this ought to be the proudest moment of your life. You have had the distinction of being shot by the great Duke of Wellington!"[20]

There is no dispute, though, as to what happened after Wellington fired. As we saw, Winchilsea pointed his pistol in the air over his head and fired a bullet that no one could have thought was aimed at the prime minister. This practice was known as "deloping." It was an indication that he did not want the duel to continue.

This business of deloping was controversial. Rule XIII of the Irish Code was quite clear: "No dumb shooting, or firing in the air, admissible *in any case*." And it went on to say with equal clarity why. "The challenger ought not to have challenged without receiving offence; and the challenged ought, if he gave offence, to have made an apology before he came on the ground: therefore *children's play* must be dishonorable on one side or the other, and is

accordingly prohibited."[21] But the gentlemen of Ireland here protested too much. It was clear enough what the point of deloping
was. A gentleman's presence at a duel indicated willingness to die
defending his honor and this established that he met one of the
criteria for being honorable. Though risking your life might show
you cared about honor, actually killing in defense of your honor
showed only that you were a good, or, at the least, a lucky, shot.
A man who put himself at risk while making no effort to defend
himself established his courage all the more clearly.

Winchilsea had actually written to his second, Lord Falmouth,
on the night before the duel, saying that he would delope. Indeed,
it was only with this understanding that Lord Falmouth was willing to participate, since he (like almost everyone else) thought that
Winchilsea owed the duke an apology. "After the first fire," Winchilsea wrote, "I shall offer the expression of regret that I shall then
be ready to make." And, though he admitted in the same note
that he should not have published the letter, he insisted, nevertheless, that he could not have apologized for doing so in the manner
proposed by Sir Henry Hardinge, because to do so "might have
subjected me to imputations which would have made life to me
utterly worthless."[22]

What were those "imputations"? The reference to Hardinge
provides the clue. For once Hardinge had written to Winchilsea on
Wellington's behalf, it was clear that he had been summoned as a
potential second. Once that had happened, Winchilsea *could* have
been thought to be apologizing merely to avoid the duel. After the
duel, Lord Falmouth offered Dr. Hume a different explanation.
Winchilsea, he said, "could not have made any apology sufficiently
adequate to the offence consistently with his character as a man of

honor without first receiving the Duke's fire."[23] On this account, Winchilsea felt that apologizing even though he was in the wrong was dishonorable, though forcing the duke into a duel, being shot at, deloping, and then apologizing, was not. Simply put: having wrongfully accused Wellington, he thought he owed the prime minister a chance to have a shot at him.

If this was indeed what he was thinking, some of his contemporaries thought he had failed to do things entirely *comme il faut*. John Cam Hobhouse, Lord Byron's friend and a radical MP, wrote in his memoirs: "I believe that it was not reckoned fair for the person accused to terminate the duel before he had exposed himself to two shots; and on the Monday following this business, as the Speaker and myself were talking it over in his library, he remarked that Lord Winchilsea had no right to fire in the air, but ought to have received the Duke's second fire. . . . The fact was, neither party gained much credit by the transaction."[24] It's part of the fascination of this duel that even Winchilsea and Falmouth didn't have a single consistent story as to what they were doing; and that others in their circle did not share their view as to what was and was not appropriate. The code was no longer working as it was supposed to.

TRADITIONAL OBJECTIONS

Given the pronounced ambivalence of British society about dueling, it's worth reflecting on the considerations that led both the law and conventional Christian morality to oppose the practice. One source of the modern European duel was what was called "judicial combat," in which members of the military ruling class, gentlemen of the rank of squire and above, could settle legal disputes by passage of arms, provided they were "granted the field" by a sufficiently important feudal lord—the Duke of Burgundy, say, or a monarch.

The popes declared their opposition to judicial combat early on: in the middle of the ninth century, Pope Nicholas I wrote a letter to the emperor Charles the Bald condemning it;[25] and the Roman Catholic Council of Trent took the trouble, in 1563, at the end of the Reformation, to fulminate, in its final session, against "the detestable custom of dueling, introduced by the contrivance of the devil, that by the bloody death of the body, he may accomplish the ruin of the soul. . . ."[26] The presupposition of this practice was that God would accord victory to the knight whose cause was just.

It was this form of combat that the Church first opposed. One objection was a matter of biblical morality. In Luke 4, verses 9 to 12, Satan placed Christ on "a pinnacle of the temple" in Jerusalem, "and said unto him, If thou be the Son of God, cast thyself down from hence":

> For it is written, He shall give his angels charge over thee, to
> keep thee: . . .
> And Jesus answering said unto him, It is said, Thou shalt
> not tempt the Lord thy God.

Christ is quoting a passage from Deuteronomy 6:16, which refers to an episode where the ancient Israelites forced God's hand by threatening to stone Moses if he didn't get Him to produce water for them in the desert. Tempting God here means something like trying to force God's hand. In judicial combat, the lord and those he granted the field were all, in a similar manner, tempting God.

The more obvious objection, however, was the violation of the sixth (or, if you are Catholic or Lutheran, the fifth) commandment: Thou shalt do no murder. In a duel over a point of honor, you set out deliberately to kill a man who has offended you or a man who has taken offense. Neither is, from a Christian point of view, sufficient reason to take someone's life.

These objections to judicial combat extended to the modern duel. The rational problem was at bottom that a duel was *about* an offense by A against B's honor, but—granted God's non-interference—its outcome depended in no way on whether A or B was in the wrong. This problem was especially evident when the offense in question was an accusation of lying. When Touchstone—the clown in Shakespeare's *As You Like It* (written around 1600)—mocks the intricacy of the duello, he does so by elaborating the processes of a quarrel between himself and "a certain courtier," which begins with the clown disparaging the courtier's beard, but only reaches an actual duel seven stages later when the courtier finally accuses the clown of lying (Act V, Sc. iv). Yet a duel does nothing to establish the truth: and being willing to respond to the "lie direct" by issuing a challenge shows only that you are willing to back up your word with your sword, whether or not what you have said is true.

A duel could establish that you were brave or foolhardy enough to fight, and so refute one particular kind of insult to a gentleman, namely, that he was a coward. But neither killing your opponent nor being killed established that you were any braver than him. Murdering another human being, an offense against the moral law, and being murdered, an offense against rational self-interest: both risks were by-products of the process. And the question was whether the ostensible aim of the duel, the protection of honor, was worth that price.

From early on there were doubters. Francis Bacon, writing in his *Charge Touching Duels* (1614), more than two centuries before Wellington challenged Winchilsea, complained, "it is a miserable effect, when young men, full of towardness and hope, such as they call *aurora filii*, sons of the morning . . . shall be cast away and destroyed in such a vain manner; but much more it is to be deplored when so much noble and gentle blood shall be spilt upon such follies. . . ."[27]

Once the duel had passed from judicial combat, which could take place only with the king's permission, to a private and illegal act, claimed as a right of the nobility, it posed a further problem: it was now *lèse majesté*. Among the great enemies of the duel, accordingly, were men like Francis Bacon and his younger French contemporary Cardinal Richelieu, who were engaged in extending the power of the state, in part by subordinating the nobility, with its independent claim to honor, to the increasingly all-embracing reach of the monarchy.

The cardinal, who was Louis XIII's chief minister, famously had the Comte de Bouteville executed in 1627, when he ignored new royal edicts underlining existing laws against dueling. (Since he had fought more than twenty duels previously, the comte was entitled to be surprised at this new insistence on the letter of an old law.) Louis, who was an enthusiast for chivalric ideals, had only reluctantly agreed to attempts at enforcing the long-standing legal ban on dueling, when Richelieu persuaded him that the cost in noble blood was too high. (In his father's reign more than eight thousand people had been killed in duels.) Lord Herbert of Cherbury, the British ambassador to Louis' court, wrote in his *Autobiography* that among "the French at that time" there was "scarce any man thought worth the looking on, that had not killed some other in a duel."[28] And the French historian and memoirist Amelot de Houssaye said that "the ordinary conversation of persons when they met in the morning was, 'Do you know who fought yesterday?' and after dinner, 'Do you know who fought this morning?'"[29]

From the point of view of the modern state, which was developing in tandem with the rise of the duel, the duel was, as Francis Bacon nicely put it, an "offence of presumption." It

> expressly gives the law an affront, as if there were two laws, one a kind of gown-law, and the other a law of reputation, as they term it, so that Paul's & Westminster, the pulpit and the courts of justice must give place to the law . . . of ordinary tables, and such reverend assemblies; the year books and statute books must give place to some French and Italian pamphlets. . . . [30]

At the time Bacon was writing, "private quarrels among great men"[31] had become distressingly common around the court of James I, and this led the king to issue an ordinance punishing not just "singular combat" at home or abroad, but also making or transmitting challenges, acting as a second, or granting the field. Bacon had been Attorney General for about a year when his *Charge Touching Duels* appeared, and it included part of his argument in a case he had brought before the Court of the Star Chamber.

In the particular case that Bacon chose to make the king's

point, there were two charges: "the one against William Priest, gentleman, for writing and sending a letter of challenge, together with a stick which should be the length of the weapon; and the other against Richard Wright esquire, for carrying and delivering the said letter and stick unto the party challenged." These two people met the minimum conditions for a duel: they were gentlemen. Bacon admitted to the judges that he "could have wished that I had met with some greater persons, as a subject for your censure."[32] Still, the matter was urgent and this case had come up. Besides, "it passeth not amiss some-times in government, that the greater sort be admonished by an example made in the meaner, and the dog to be beaten before the lion." Already, in the early seventeenth century, the duel is an equalizing institution, and it is Bacon, speaking against it, who is insisting upon distinctions of rank among gentlemen.

THE ENLIGHTENMENT DEBATE

For us today, the most obvious argument for permitting dueling is probably that it is the free act of willing participants. The first person I know of who makes essentially this suggestion is William Hazlitt, the great English essayist and critic; writing, probably, a year or two before Wellington's duel, he opined that dueling should be legal because it involved, to use a modern formulation, consenting adults.[33] But it was too radical an idea at the turn of the nineteenth century to withdraw legislation against bad behavior just because it only harmed volunteers.

The best defense of the duel available within the intellectual frameworks of the time runs parallel to the Utilitarian theory of punishment. "All punishment," as Jeremy Bentham, the great Utilitarian philosopher-reformer, wrote in 1823, "in itself is evil."[34] So it might at first seem that when we punish people, we are only adding a new evil to the evil they have already done. But, as Bentham went on to argue, a world with the institution of punishment, properly advertised and administered, is a world free of other evils that we could not escape without it. Provided the evil of punishment is outweighed by the evils it deters, we may rationally support it for that reason.

Consider now the duel. A society of people who treat each other with respect, where reputations are not sullied by lies—where, in a formula, gentlemen mind their manners—is preferable to one where they do not. The institution of the duel provides a rather compelling incentive for gentlemen to mind their manners. But the duel is unlike punishment in one important respect. You can defend punishment as a deterrent because it is a practice enforced by public institutions for the general good. By contrast, for dueling, which is a private practice, to do its work, duelists have to believe that it serves some end of their own, since encouraging third parties to be honorable is not something for which most people would ordinarily be willing to risk their lives. Why should I enter into mortal combat with you in order to keep other people polite? The sense of honor gives men just such private reasons for dueling. From within the institution, the reason for making and responding to challenges is obvious: if you don't, you will lose your right to the respect of your fellows. Still, to justify dueling because it deters discourtesy is to take a perspective from outside the world of honor.

Something like this argument was often made in the eighteenth century, though, frequently by men who agreed that the practice was immoral or irrational or both. In his *History of the Reign of the Emperor Charles V*, the Scottish historian and divine Dr. William Robertson, principal of Edinburgh University, wrote that the practice was "not justified by any principle of reason," but, he went on,

> it must be admitted that to this absurd custom, we must ascribe in some degree the extraordinary gentleness and complaisance of modern manners, and that respectful attention of one man to another, which at present render the social intercourses of life far more agreeable and decent, than among the most civilized nations of antiquity.[35]

This Enlightenment commonplace—that the duel is un-Christian and unreasonable yet does, at least, improve manners—had clearly irritated the leading philosopher of the Scottish Enlightenment, David Hume. For in 1742, he added a discussion of dueling to his essay "Of the Rise and Progress of the Arts and Sciences," aimed at refuting the claim that the institution was useful "for the refining of manners."

Hume is scathing in his rebuttal: "conversation, among the greatest rustics, is not commonly invested with such rudeness as can give occasion to duels," he says. And he objects that, in distinguishing the man of honor from the man of virtue—in recognizing a normative system of honor distinct from morality—the honor code allows "debauchees" and "spendthrifts" to keep their place in a society that should repudiate them.[36]

In the same year, Francis Hutcheson—the father, it is conventional to say, of the Scottish Enlightenment—condemns dueling in his textbook *Philosophiae Moralis Institutio Compendiaria* (translated in 1745 as *A Short Introduction to Moral Philosophy*). For lies and libels, the duel is too cruel a response: "death is too grievous a punishment for opprobrious words." And, in any case, "the fortune of the combat is as blind and capricious as any."[37]

Indeed, given the unreliability of the eighteenth-century dueling pistol, firing at each other at the normal distance of twelve to fifteen yards amounted in most cases to leaving the outcome to chance. Joseph Hamilton in his well-known *Duelling Handbook*, which appeared soon after Wellington's duel, quotes "a celebrated writer" who made this point sharply with a persuasive analogy:

> If having seized a man who has murdered my wife, I should carry him before a tribunal, and demand justice, what should we think of that judge, if he should order that the criminal and I should cast lots which of us should be hanged.[38]

Adam Smith, in his *Lectures on Jurisprudence* (1762), argues that duels persist because the law does not protect men sufficiently from the affronts to honor that lead to challenges: he suggests that this is a deficiency of the law. "As the injury done was with a design to expose the person and make him ridiculous, so the proper punishment would be to make the person who injured the other as ridiculous as he had made him, by exposing to shame in the pillory, and by imprisonment or fine, arbitrarily adapted to the circumstances of the affront."[39] Smith is here insisting on a point that Hutcheson had made: it is up to the government to make sure that the law provides a sufficient remedy for the harms for which gentlemen seek satisfaction. If the "civil governors" have not done this, Hutcheson says, the "larger share of the guilt" of the duel lies with them. Smith, like Hume, does not put much effort into arguing that the duel is bad in itself. That is left, as I say, to an introductory philosophy textbook.

William Godwin, the eighteenth-century philosophical analyst, in an appendix to his *Enquiry Concerning Political Justice* (1793) on dueling, focuses not on questioning whether it is irrational and wrong—this he, too, takes for granted—but rather on showing that it takes more courage to resist a challenge than to accept it. "Which of these two actions is the truest test of courage," he asks, "the engaging in a practice which our judgment disapproves, because we cannot submit to the consequences of following that judgment; or the doing what we believe to be right, and cheerfully encountering all the consequences that may be annexed to the practice of virtue?"[40] So here, in effect, he couched an argument against dueling in the language of honor. Even Dr. Johnson, who could hardly be said to be an enthusiast for the Enlightenment, conceded to James Boswell, in one of the discussions of dueling they had in the Hebrides, that "he fairly owned that he could not explain" the "rationality" of the duel.[41] When Voltaire remarked—in an aside in the *Philosophical Dictionary*—that dueling is "forbidden by reason, by religion, and by all the laws," he was reporting an intellectual consensus.[42]

But we misunderstand this consensus if we fail to see how much these gentlemen also felt the lure of honor. In his *History of England*, Hume says that dueling has "shed much of the best blood in Christendom during more than two centuries," but he finds himself conceding that the "absurd" maxims underlying the duel are nevertheless "generous" (i.e., noble); and he points out that, "notwithstanding the severity of law and authority of reason, such is the prevailing force of custom, they are far from being entirely exploded."[43] Smith believes that the duel is a response to a genuine affront. Hutcheson is not denying that there are important stakes in the duel; he is only insisting that the duel is not a reasonable way of pursuing them.

There is little evidence that their arguments made much headway among gentlemen. James Boswell—not only Johnson's biographer but also a Scottish gentleman of rank (he was ninth laird of Auchinleck)—contemplated accepting a number of challenges, even though he had forced Johnson to admit they were irrational; and his son, Sir Alexander Boswell, was one of the last victims of the duel in Scotland, dying in March 1822 after a duel at Auchtertool in Fife.

But Boswell père captured the conflict between Christian duty and the laws of honor as clearly as anyone in one of the many fascinating footnotes to his *Life of Johnson*:

> It must be confessed, that, from the prevalent notions of honor, a gentleman who receives a challenge is reduced to a dreadful alternative. A remarkable instance of this is furnished by a clause in the will of the late Colonel Thomas, of the Guards, written the night before he fell in a duel, September 3, 1783: "In the first place, I commit my soul to Almighty God, in hopes of his mercy and pardon for the irreligious step I now (in compliance with the unwarrantable customs of this wicked world) put myself under the necessity of taking."[44]

If cogent rational and moral argument failed in their efforts to weaken the institution, what succeeded? The aftermath of the Wellington-Winchilsea affair is suggestive.

THE AFTERMATH

Once Winchilsea fired his gun into the air and so satisfied his somewhat eccentric sense of the proprieties, his written expression of contrition, which had been drafted before the duel began, was presented to Wellington through the seconds. Wellington's response was: "This won't do. This is no apology." Hardinge insisted that they would have to continue firing unless the document was amended to make it clear that Winchilsea was apologizing. It was at this point that Dr. Hume made the splendidly useful suggestion that the actual word "apology" be inserted. Winchilsea and Falmouth complied. Dr. Hume witnessed the revised document. It included a promise, on Winchilsea's part, to print the text of the apology in the *Standard*, in the very pages where he had published the accusation that had led to Wellington's challenge.

Not surprisingly, these events were soon the talk of London. Many people professed themselves shocked that the prime minister had taken part in a duel. *The Times* declared that the duel had been quite unnecessary. The *Morning Herald* observed sententiously: "No wonder the multitude break laws when the law makers themselves, the great, the powerful and the famous, set them at open defiance."[45] But others wondered at the great man's participation not so much because it was illegal as because it made him look, well, ridiculous. An anonymous cartoonist published an image of the five men, with Winchilsea dancing on an anti-

Catholic petition as the duke shoots off the tail of his coat. Under Wellington runs the verse:

> *The D-ke when marshaled in the tented field,*
> *To no aspiring enemy would deign to yield;*
> *Shall he when dignified by royal favor*
> *Submit to insult by each—?—no never!*

Below Winchilsea we read: "The fundamental doctrines of Christianity subverted."[46] In the background, Falmouth proffers a paper to Hardinge, on which is written the single word: "Apology." The overall effect is, indeed, comical.

Newspaper comments and cartoons like these were of crucial significance in the changing response to the duel. The rise of a popular press and of working-class literacy made it increasingly clear—and, as democratic sentiment grew, increasingly unacceptable—that gentlemen were living outside the law. When dueling was an aristocratic practice known mostly only within the class of those who practiced it, there was no place for the attitudes of ordinary people to shape its honor world. The modern press brought all the citizens of Britain into a single community of knowledge and evaluation.[47]

Despite this gentle mockery, Wellington clearly got the better of the affair. Hardinge had expressed grim indignation on Battersea Fields at Winchilsea's refusal to apologize when he was so clearly in the wrong. That was the essence of a protest he read once the principals were in their positions. In exchanges with Falmouth both before and after the duel, Hardinge stressed each time the impropriety, in his view, of having imposed on the duke the neces-

"King's Colledge [*sic*] to wit—a practical essay." Anon. (perhaps Thomas Howell Jones). Published by S. W. Fores, 41 Piccadilly, 1829. British Cartoon Archive, University of Kent, www.cartoons.ac.uk. (The attribution to Jones comes from the Web site of King's College London: http://www.kcl.ac.uk/depsta/iss/archives/wellington/duel17.htm.)

sity of an exchange of fire. Lord Falmouth's frantic attempts to get Hardinge and Wellington and even Dr. Hume to acknowledge his reasons for agreeing to act as Winchilsea's second reflected his awareness that they thought his participation unworthy.

Hardinge's speech before the duel is a splendid exercise in condescension. After insisting to Winchilsea and Falmouth that they alone were responsible for the fact that the dispute had reached this extreme outcome, he told them that they alone would have to bear responsibility for the consequences. And he ended by saying, "if I do not now express my opinion to your lordships in the same terms of disgust I have done in the progress of the affair, it is because I wish to imitate the moderation of the Duke of Wellington." (Of course, saying you are refraining from calling someone's behavior disgusting is just a roundabout way of expressing your disgust. Dr. Hume recorded that he heard Winchilsea mutter something in response about "rather strong language.") When Falmouth tried, once more, to justify Winchilsea's persistence in the duel, Hardinge cut him off even more contemptuously: "Indeed, my Lord Falmouth," he said, "I do not envy you your feelings." You can almost hear him restraining a sneer.

In Dr. Hume's narration, Falmouth's increasing agitation contrasts with Hardinge's solid correctness. By the end, Falmouth—the doctor is not quite sure—may have tears in his eyes. Hardinge's position is straightforward: as a man of honor, the duke believed he had no choice but to issue his challenge, but it was a contemptible thing to have forced this upon him.

The latter sentiment—indignation at Winchilea's refusal to obviate the duel with an apology—was widely shared. Charles Greville's summary of the response (at least in his elevated circles) is straightforward: "Nothing could equal the astonishment caused by this event. Everybody, of course, sees the event in a different light; all blame Lord Winchilsea, but they are divided as to whether the Duke ought to have fought or not." Perhaps Greville's most striking contribution was his description of Winchilsea as a "maniac."[48]

Yet something had changed. A generation earlier, there could have been no doubt that Wellington was doing what he had to. Few passages of the prose written at the time can have more clearly displayed the tension between the culture of honor and the new world that was emerging than Charles Greville's frank personal evaluation—written, I should point out, for publication only after his death—of Wellington's decision to issue his challenge to Winchilsea.

> I think the Duke ought not to have challenged him; it was very juvenile, and he stands in too high a position, and his life is so much *publica cura* that he should have treated him and his letter with the contempt they merited; it was a great error in judgment, but certainly a venial one, for it is impossible not to admire the high spirit which disdained to shelter itself behind the immunities of his great character and station, and the simplicity, and almost humility, which made him at once descend to the level of Lord Winchilsea, when he might, without subjecting himself to any imputation derogatory to his honor, have assumed a tone of lofty superiority and treated him as unworthy of notice. Still, it was beneath his dignity; it lowered him, and was more or less ridiculous.[49]

Is Greville committed to the ideology of the duel? The duke was ignoring the obvious risk to the public interest in hazarding his own life. The challenge, Greville says, was "juvenile," "ridiculous," yet the error in making it, he insists, was "venial." In the world of honor, though, making yourself ridiculous, acting beneath your dignity, is a mortal sin. Where Greville's defection from the old culture of the duel shows most is in his ignoring the principle that, on the field, all gentlemen are equal. Rule XXXVIII of the Royal Code, which William Hamilton proposed in the *Duelling Handbook* mentioned earlier, is clear: "The parties . . . have, by the very act of meeting, made an acknowledgment of equality. . . ."

And, though this Code was a novelty, another early nineteenth-century attempt to temper the extremes of the duel, this element of it was thoroughly traditional. If there were social ranks even among gentlemen—every member of the House of Lords had a place in an order of precedence—there was also, as I have insisted, an important sense in which they belonged to a single stratum: that is presumably why peers are called peers. In the world of honor, the equality of gentlemen, displayed in the duel, declared their shared superiority to the common people. Deny this and the whole scheme begins to fall apart.

Greville's doubts about whether Wellington should have asked Winchilsea for satisfaction reflected a certain tension in the codes of gentlemanly behavior. On the one hand, there was a distinctly hierarchical insistence on the inferiority of the "lower orders"; on the other hand, there was an egalitarianism within the ranks of gentlemen. When Greville said that the earl wasn't on the duke's level—so that the duke was "lowering himself" by treating him as an equal—whatever he meant by "level," he was appealing to an inappropriate standard. And, indeed, in rejecting the ideal of a form of equality that connected the grandest duke to the merest country squire, he was rejecting this one progressive feature of the dying code. In the culture of the duel, any gentleman—and nobody could deny that Winchilsea was that—was worthy of notice. Greville judged Wellington's encounter juvenile by a standard other than the gentlemanly honor that had long sustained the practice.

King George, it should be said, showed no such ambivalence. He continued in a long European tradition of royal toleration of the nobility's propensity for flouting laws that were supposed to reflect the sovereign's will. Wellington was at Windsor by midday to report at court on what had happened. Greville tells us that the king was "highly pleased with the Winchilsea affair."[50] According to the editor of the *Literary Gazette*, His Majesty supposed that, given Wellington's sensitivity, "being a soldier . . . the course pursued had been unavoidable."[51] Military gentlemen, the king knew, occupied a defining place in the world of honor. And, perhaps for this reason, the opinion of many ordinary men and women seems to have swung behind Wellington, too; as the Duchess of Wellington told her son, whereas before "the Mob were . . . abusing your father, now they are cheering him again."[52]

This was almost certainly just what her husband had planned. In the heady atmosphere of constitutional debate, as popular discontent seethed in England as well as in Ireland, Wellington's conversion to Catholic emancipation had worried many of his conservative fellow citizens. Many aspersions had been cast against him. In picking the eccentric earl and his preposterous allegation to stand for his detractors, Wellington had made a shrewd choice. Writing to the Duke of Buckingham a month after the duel, Wellington claimed—it is halfway between an admission and a boast—that when Winchilsea's "furious letter" was published, "I immediately perceived the advantage it gave me."

The duel, for Wellington, as for Winchilsea, was an attempt to shape public opinion, though the stakes for the duke were predictably grander. He was seeking, he said, to shift public sympathy toward himself in the face of innuendo and rumor from those who opposed his political decision. And, on his account, he had been entirely successful. Winchilsea had played into his hands. He had made a preposterous allegation, offensively declined to withdraw it, and then forced the duke to stake his life. Through it all the prime minister sought to make it appear that he was doing, as usual, only what duty required. "The atmosphere of calumny in which I had been for some time living cleared away. . . . I am satisfied," he concluded, "that the public interests at the moment required that I should do what I did."[53]

Perhaps Wellington's own account, if we take it at face value, represents the most scandalous defection of all. What had seemed a reluctant defense of personal honor is recast, in this letter, in cold-blooded, instrumental terms—as a matter of political calculation, even manipulation. The purest embodiment of the honor code has, it would seem, been recruited for ordinary political ends.

WHAT KILLED THE DUEL?

So how was it that the duel itself eventually fell into contempt? How did a set of norms weaken sufficiently that an aristocrat like Charles Cavendish Fulke Greville could see the duke's act as "juvenile"? We've seen some of the elements. The rise of the administrative state, with its concern for orderly legality. A popular press that turned an in-group institution into a spectacle for mirthful outsiders. The weakening grip of the gentlemanly creed of equality-within-superiority. But might these be symptoms of a larger shift?

One powerful suggestion—made in the work of V. G. Kiernan, the preeminent historian of the European duel—is that the class whose norm it was gradually lost its central place in British public life. The ruling aristocracy was being superseded in the early nineteenth century, as Marx famously argued, by a new class; men like Peel whose family fortunes had been made in what the aristocrats disparaged as "trade." New state bureaucracies were developing, with new tools, such as statistics, run by a growing and increasingly professionalized class of officials.

Businessmen believe in being businesslike; and bureaucrats famously prefer things orderly, too. Many in these new classes favored parliamentary reform: they wanted to deny the landed gentry their traditional rights to allocate seats in the Commons, to stop vote buying, and to extend the franchise. The Catholic Relief Act was one of the many tactical sallies and retreats in that battle. While allowing Catholics into Parliament, the bill increased the property requirements for voting for county seats in Ireland fivefold, from forty shillings (which is what it had been in England for nearly four hundred years) to ten pounds, thus contributing to the pressures for electoral reform that were to culminate in the disturbances that led to the passage of the Great Reform Bill a mere three years later, in 1832.

The tension between honor and legality must have been especially strong for Wellington because he was not only a professional soldier but also a public administrator of long service, in a family of public administrators. His elder brother, the Marquess Wellesley, was one of the leading public servants of the age. He had been Governor–General of India, Ambassador to Spain during the Peninsula Wars, and foreign secretary. William, the second son of their father, the Earl of Mornington, had also been Secretary for Ireland, and he was later Master of the Mint under Lord Liverpool, joining his brothers as Lord Maryborough in the Lords in 1821, where their youngest brother Henry, who had been Ambassador to France, also arrived in 1828, as Lord Cowley.

The duke himself—aside from his extraordinary military

career—had been Ambassador to France, first Plenipotentiary at the Congress of Vienna, and a member of the Privy Council since 1807, as well, of course, as Chief Secretary for Ireland; and he had entered the Irish Parliament as an MP at the age of twenty-one. As aristocrats with military connections, the Wellesleys might have been favorable to the duel; as public servants, they had the same reasons that Bacon and Richelieu had to oppose it.

Francis Bacon anticipated the mechanism of the duel's demise, when the modern duel was just beginning, in his address to the court in *Charge Touching Duels*:

> I should think (my Lords) that men of birth and quality will leave the practice, when it begins to . . . come so low as to barber-surgeons and butchers, and such base mechanical persons.[54]

A duel was an affair of honor. It depended on the existence of a powerful class whose members could establish their status by getting away with a practice contrary to law that others could not. It was a further sign of the diminishing status of that class when, in the first decades of the nineteenth century, duels began to take place more frequently between people who, if they were gentlemen at all, were so by virtue of their membership in the professions or their success in trade. Once "base mechanical" persons could contemplate engaging in it, the duel's capacity to bring distinction was exhausted.

Bacon's is the view in prospect, as the duel is rising toward its eighteenth-century apogee. For a retrospect, listen to Richard Cobden, the great Liberal parliamentarian, in a speech in Rochdale in 1859, recalling when dueling was a regular "mode of meeting a certain description of insult." Cobden tells the electors of Rochdale:

> Well, I remember that some linendrapers' assistants took it into their heads to go down one Sunday morning . . . and they began fighting duels; and that as soon as the linendrapers' assistants took to dueling, it became very infamous in the eyes of the upper classes. . . . Now nothing would be so ridiculous as any nobleman or gentleman thinking of resenting an insult by going out and fighting a duel about it.[55]

Cobden's view was that Bacon's prediction had been confirmed, however belatedly: the adoption of dueling by "base men" had led to its relinquishment by the aristocracy. And his mocking tone reminds us that in an increasingly democratic age, the duel was an unloved symbol of aristocratic privilege. Oscar Wilde said famously that so long as war was regarded as wicked, it would always have its fascination. "When it is looked upon as vulgar," he went on, "it will cease to be popular." Much the same might be said of the duel; and we might add that it was the increasing vulgarity of the duel that finally made its wickedness perspicuous. As long as the institution was merely condemned, as mad or bad, it could flourish; only when it was contemned did it falter.

Three years after his duel, in the "Days of May"—May 7–15, 1832—Wellington was unable to form a government for William IV, the new king. The duke's resistance to electoral reform—or rather the resistance of many conservatives like him in the Lords—

had led England to the brink of revolution. As rioting spread across the realm, the old aristocrat had to witness the concessions of the Great Reform Act, which marked the earliest steps toward the end of the supremacy of the House of Lords and the beginning of the rise of a House of Commons, now more representative of a new commercial and professional middle class. As John Stuart Mill wrote in 1840, "the government of England is progressively changing from the government of a few, to the government, not indeed of the many, but of many;—from an aristocracy with a popular infusion, to the régime of the middle class."[56]

Many of the new men shared the Evangelical convictions of William Wilberforce, who had worked for decades not just on anti-slavery and public morals—including the campaign against dueling—but also on parliamentary reform. Wellington and many of his peers were persuaded not to oppose the bill by the king's threat—under the insistent pressure of Earl Grey and his cabinet—to create enough new peers to outvote them. And when the new Parliament met, His Grace is supposed to have observed that he "never saw so many shocking bad hats in his life." These peevishly snobbish words, like the duel with Winchilsea, reflect the gap between his sentiments and the spirit of the times. Writing in 1865, at the end of a long life, Byron's friend John Cam Hobhouse remarked of Wellington's decision, "It is difficult at this time of day, so many years since the change of opinion, and of usage, in regard to dueling, to give an impartial judgment on this transaction." But, he continued, as if reporting the practices of an alien culture, "Dueling, like bull-baiting, prize-fighting, cock-fighting, and other barbarous usages, had its rules, which could not be transgressed without some amount of censure. . . ."[57]

THE LAST DUELS

The changes I have been discussing occurred in Great Britain. In different places—the United States, Russia, Germany, Spain— dueling came to an end in different ways, as you'd expect, given the variety of the social and political contexts in these different societies. Honor did not disappear with dueling, of course, in the British Isles or anywhere else. But after centuries of trying, the bureaucrats, whose complaints we heard in Bacon's *Charge*, have had their way. Perhaps nothing displays the changing meaning of the word "gentleman" more sharply than the fact that Cardinal Newman did not feel it preposterous to say in 1852: "It is almost a definition of a gentleman to say he is one who never inflicts pain."[58] If that is what a gentleman is, nothing could be more ungentlemanly than the duel.

By the middle of the nineteenth century, honor could no longer be protected by the duel in the British Isles. James Kelly, the author of a history of Irish dueling, identifies a Captain Smith who was shot and killed in 1833 in Fermoy "following an 'angry discussion' over the relative merits of various regiments"; and Lord Londonderry and the Lord Mayor of Dublin and their opponents each emerged unscathed from the field later in the 1830s.[59] After them, the records fizzle out.

The last gentleman to be prosecuted for dueling in Scotland took the field in August 1826; he was a reluctant duelist, a Kirkcaldy linen merchant (a tradesman, Wellington might have insisted), and the opponent who forced him to his challenge was his banker, an ex-military officer. The banker died; the businessman was acquitted.[60]

And perhaps the last time a gentleman shot another on the field of honor in England was in 1852, when George Smythe (Disraeli's friend and the model for Coningsby) and a Colonel Romilly, both of them members of Parliament for Canterbury, met over an election dispute in what is often said to be the last duel in England.[61] It was, Kiernan tells us, "an appropriately burlesque event, with the two men and their seconds having to share the station fly at Weybridge." There is, indeed, something comical in the image of two gentlemen and their seconds getting off the train to share a taxi to a field where they plan to shoot at each other. As one contemporary observed: "The incident was dealt with in a witty article in the *Times*, and so ridicule at last did more than morality to kill dueling. *Solventur risu tabulae*."[62] The case is dismissed with laughter.

My own favorite among the last duels in England occurred when Sir William Gregory, husband of Lady Gregory, the well-known Irish literary figure, took to the field at Osterley Park in 1851 against another member of the Turf Club, in a rather complicated dispute over the concealment of the ownership of a horse. Writing much later, Sir William prefaces his account by saying that he wants his son to understand why he came to do something "so foolish, so wrong, and so contrary to public opinion."[63] The description of the duel—which was delayed a few days to allow him to collect his winnings from a horse race—is bound to strike a contemporary reader as unintentionally hilarious. At one point, Gregory's second, Sir Robert Peel, a son of the recently deceased prime minister, wonders out loud whether death is the appropriate penalty for lying about a horse. A moment earlier he observes, "Of course, . . . if we escape hanging, we shall have to live abroad for the rest of our lives," and, Gregory tells us, they "discussed our future residence." One hopes that Sir William's son Robert Gregory (whose death in the First World War was the occasion of Yeats's "An Irish Airman Foresees His Death") was indeed edified by this narrative.

When Guy Crouchback in Evelyn Waugh's Second World War novel *Officers and Gentlemen* is asked what he would do if someone challenged him to a duel, his laconic answer is: "Laugh."[64] So it was at the end of the process; but the laughter was already beginning when the great Duke of Wellington was mocked for challenging that "maniac," the Earl of Winchilsea and of Nottingham.

TWO

FREEING CHINESE FEET

There is nothing which makes us objects of ridicule so much as footbinding.

—Kang Youwei[1]

A MEMORANDUM TO THE THRONE

In 1898, a Chinese intellectual named Kang Youwei sent a memorandum to the Imperial Palace in Beijing about footbinding. There was nothing unusual in this. The empire had been run for centuries by educated literati, selected in highly competitive exams, who governed locally as magistrates—the mandarins—in the counties of China. Those who did best in this tiered exam system—they were known as *jinshi*—were called to Beijing to work in the government or (if they did especially well) to serve in the Hanlin Academy, where they studied the Confucian classics and applied their lessons to the problems of the day. The literati communicated with the emperors through memoranda like Kang's (conventionally called "memorials"), which were written in an elegant classical prose and percolated slowly upwards through the bureaucracy. If a memorial was deemed of sufficient importance, it might actually reach the palace, either directly or reshaped into proposals that the emperor could finally issue as the edicts that governed the imperial system.

Kang was a leading member of a group of late nineteenth-century literati who, though immersed in the ancient Confucian classics,were nevertheless convinced that China needed modernizing. Unlike the conservatives who ran the national bureaucracy they believed that, in bringing their country into the new era, there was much to be learned from the West. Kang himself was a supporter of the Qing monarchy, but he also believed that it needed constitutional change.

Behind all the intricate formality of the imperial system of those days, one central fact was clear: at the center of the maze was Cixi, the dowager empress. She was by any standards an extraordinary woman. She had arrived in the Forbidden City, the imperial enclave at the heart of Beijing, in the summer of 1852, at the age of sixteen, to become one of the many concubines of the new emperor. For more than two hundred years a foreign dynasty from Manchuria had been ruling in China and the new Xianfeng Emperor was the eighth Qing ruler. Two years earlier, his predecessor had died, and now, after a suitable period of mourning, it was time for the twenty-one-year-old monarch to begin building his collection of concubines.

Sixty Manchu girls were chosen that year from the thousands whose names were submitted from every part of the empire, on the basis of lists reviewed by local officials and passed on to the capital. These lists provided a description of each girl's ancestry, along with an astrological analysis based on her date of birth, and a description of her character and education and her looks.

It was the duty of the widow of the late emperor (the then dowager empress) to review the new concubines and to classify them; and she does not seem to have been especially impressed with the new girl, since Cixi was placed in the lower ranks of the concubines. It was only three years later that she was summoned to the imperial bedchamber to perform her allotted function for the Xianfeng Emperor for the first time.

Unlike the dowager empress, the emperor apparently took to the young woman almost immediately, and from that moment she began a meteoric rise in influence as well as in rank. By 1856, she had given the emperor his first and only son; a year later, when the boy reached the age of one, she received an imperial rank just below that of the empress Ci'an.

When her husband died in 1861, her son, the new emperor, was only five. And so the empire entered a period in which power was shared officially between Cixi and the dowager empress Ci'an, on the one hand, and a group of male regents, on the other. (The two women were known as the East and West Empress Dowager, because they lived in the east and the west of the Forbidden City.)

In the complex political struggles that ensued, Cixi, with her sharp grasp of power and her mastery of shifting allegiances, gradually established preeminence. After her son's early death from smallpox, she placed her four-year-old nephew on the throne as the Guangxu Emperor. There is something of an irony in the fact that *Guangxu* means "glorious succession," since the new emperor was of the same generation as his predecessor, which was a breach of Manchu tradition. Indeed, the boy's main claim to the title seems to have been his father's support for Cixi in the intrigues of the court.

Cixi was beautiful, charismatic, intelligent, and amusing; Sir Robert Hart, an Irishman who served as Inspector-General of the Chinese Customs from 1863 to 1911, said she spoke "in a very pleasant feminine voice."[2] She herself once said, later in life, that many people were jealous of her in her youth "because I was considered to be a beautiful woman at that time."[3] In the brilliant yellow silk robes of the imperial rank, with details embroidered in black, red, green, and blue, she was an impressive figure, even though (like Queen Victoria, who ruled that other empire which challenged her from across the globe) she was only five feet tall.

From the death of her husband until her own death nearly half a century later, Cixi ruled—for all but a hundred days—as the Chinese phrase had it, from "behind the curtains." At any particular time, there were Manchu princes in the palace who had the most influence on her and on the nation. When the direction of the government changed, it was because she shifted her support from one group to another. As China learned to deal with the increasing encroachments of outside powers, this diminutive woman had what it took to survive every challenge to her authority from within; but her judgment of the world outside was less certain.

In 1889, the Guangxu Emperor—in whose name Cixi had been ruling—reached the age of eighteen and began to rule, at least officially, himself. (Even this was a reflection of the empress's power: he should by tradition have broken free of his regent at the age of sixteen.) In fact, though, the dowager empress was still close to the levers of power. In April 1895, China suffered a naval defeat to Japan, and was forced to sign the humiliating Treaty of Shimonoseki. That was the year that Kang, along with many other bright, young scholars, arrived in Beijing, at the age of thirty-seven, to take the *jinshi* examinations. But even before he actually sat for the exams, he broke protocol by memorializing the throne, drafting a 10,000-word petition, which was signed by hundreds of the other provincial-exam degree holders—the *juren*—who had gathered like him to take the more demanding *jinshi* exam.

The petitioners urged the throne to resist Japan and proposed massive social, economic, and political reforms. Their ambitions for their country were frustrated for several years by the senior members of the bureaucracy. Though the emperor seemed to be aware that serious change was needed, he apparently did not have enough power or independence from the dowager empress, or the more conservative Manchu aristocrats she supported, to overrule the officials who were supposed to be advising him.

Then, for a period of about one hundred days, between June 11 and September 21, 1898, the emperor began to initiate real reforms, inspired in good measure by other memorials from Kang Youwei.[4] For those Hundred Days, the empress dowager watched while the emperor issued forty or so decrees. He abolished the famous "eight-legged essay"—the long-established highly for-mulaic prose form of the traditional exam system.[5] He sought to open education to Western science, and to the study of modern commerce, engineering, and mining. He proposed reform of the archaic budget process; strengthening the navy. He dismissed recalcitrant senior officials. And—as a naive but admiring British missionary living in Beijing at the time put it—he sought "to abol-ish useless offices both in Peking and the provinces."[6]

The emperor even met with Kang, a mere junior official in the Board of Trade, which was almost unprecedented. Encouraged, Kang sent a great flood of writings toward the palace in the Hun-dred Days, transmitted under the authority of various senior offi-cials, and sometimes, it seems, through secret unofficial channels. (Kang's friendship with Weng Tonghe, the Guangxu Emperor's tutor, was an important factor.)[7]

In the midst of these epic events, Kang found time to argue in his footbinding memorial that changing the status of women was central to China's reformation.[8] For him, clearly, this was an issue of major importance. And he summarized in a few pages the argument that the throne should begin by banning the binding of women's feet.

Kang's memorial compares Chinese, to their disadvantage, to foreigners. "I look at Europeans and Americans," he wrote, "so strong and vigorous because their mothers do not bind feet and therefore have strong offspring. Now that we must compete with other nations, to transmit weak offspring is perilous."[9] But a central theme of his argument had to do with the damage done by footbinding to China's national reputation. "All countries have international relations, and they compare their political institutions with one another" he began, "so that if one commits the slightest error the others ridicule and look down upon it." And he went on:

> It is no longer the time when we were united under one rule and isolated from the whole world. Now China is narrow and crowded, has opium addicts and streets lined with beggars. Foreigners have been taking pictures and laughing at us for these things and criticizing us for being barbarians. There is nothing which makes us objects of ridicule so much as footbinding. I, your humble servant, feel deeply ashamed at heart.[10]

It was to be another four years before Cixi finally issued an edict urging the end of footbinding. In the interim, a great deal had happened; and, as we shall see, Kang's memorandum played no role in the decision. But though Kang's memorandum failed, his argument—that footbinding was a blot on the national escutcheon—succeeded. It succeeded because his concern for national honor was shared by many in the educated classes who shaped China's transformation from an empire into a modern state.

The literati, whose predecessors had shaped the world of the empire for more than two thousand years, were as crucial in the dissolution of immemorial traditions as they had been in maintaining them. I want to explore the process that led Kang and his confreres to their conviction that China's honor demanded an end to this ancient tradition. The revolution they began, which brought to an end a practice that had shaped the life of the Chinese elite for about a millennium, is the second of my moral revolutions.

HONOR AND IDENTITY

We began our exploration of honor with the duel, in which individual honor is at stake. A gentleman took the field, in the usual case, to defend his own honor. But gentlemen also issued challenges in defense of the honor of ladies; mothers, sisters, daughters, lovers, wives, and sometimes (in earlier days) ladies allied with their liege lord. They pledged their honor to defend a lady's; they impugned the honor of the gentleman they challenged, because he had shamed a lady and breached thereby the code of honor; they salvaged her honor by disgracing the source of her shame. As a result the system of honor could make demands on you even when you had done nothing and nothing had been done to you. Honor is not, even in this simple way, merely personal.

Indeed, your honor is intimately associated in many ways with those aspects of your identity that derive from membership in social groups. As we saw in the last chapter, you fight even the duel for personal honor *as* a gentleman. Only gentlemen can issue challenges, only gentlemen can accept them. And, in general, a gentleman's entitlement to the respect of other gentlemen (and of ladies) depends on conformity to a code that makes quite specific demands. Break the code and you lose the right to be respected. Collective identities shape individual honor because respect and contempt for individuals is molded by the ways we think of them as belonging to various social kinds.

So, one way that identity matters is when it determines what the codes of honor require of you. (I shall sometimes call the things that honor requires or permits you to do *honor practices*.) The most obvious examples have to do with gender. Whether you are a man or a woman often plays a crucial role in determining what the codes of honor demand of you, what behavior on your part commands (or loses) respect. Class matters very often, too. In eighteenth-century England, the codes required men of the upper classes to answer challenges to a duel from other gentlemen. In nineteenth-century China, they required women of the upper classes to have their feet bound. In the case of each of these codes, how you were supposed to behave depended on your rank and your gender; and the identities of others shaped how you should treat them. An honorable man married a foot-bound woman; a foot-bound woman would not be married to a man without honor. A gentleman accepted challenges to a duel from other gentlemen, but not from men of the "lower orders" . . . and certainly not from women. The penalty in every case for breaches of these codes was the loss of honor, which means, as we have seen, the loss of the entitlement to respect.

Where a system of honor is based on esteem (and not just on recognition), the distribution of esteem is comparative. This is obvious enough where the standard that underlies esteem is military prowess, as it was in Wellington's professional culture of honor. But judgments of esteem, whatever the standard, almost always entail comparison to what the philosophers Geoffrey Brennan and Philip Pettit call a "reference group."[11] Suppose I esteem you for being kind as a nurse. The degree of kindness that merits esteem in a nurse may be lower than the self-sacrificing kindness of a loving parent and higher than the kindness of an ordinary Good Samaritan. Whether you have done well by the standard appropriate to your group will depend on what the normal expectations are about how members of that group should behave.

Not only does your social identity determine what codes you must conform to, then, it also fixes those with whom you are competing for honor. In effect, honor works to reward those who are particularly estimable among those in their particular social group. It rewards those who do more than they must; and thus provides incentives for people to go "above and beyond the call of duty."

But there's an equally important—and totally distinct—way that identity matters to honor: we may *share* the honor or dishonor of those with whom we share an identity. When Shakespeare's Henry V—at the siege of the port city of Harfleur in 1415—asks his followers to "cry 'God for Harry, England and St. George,' " they know that their leader carries not just his own honor but also the honor of his country into the field.

> *On, on, you noblest English . . .*
> *Dishonor not your mothers; now attest*
> *That those whom you call'd fathers did beget you (Act III,*
> *   Sc. i)*

he says, reminding them that they, like him, have their honor and the nation's honor in their care. Ordinary Englishmen in the battle ranks, peasant soldiers who were not themselves noble at all, could share in honor through their participation in the assault on the walled town of Harfleur *as* soldiers. At the battle of Agincourt, which took place a couple of months later, the king makes it explicit:

> *We few, we happy few, we band of brothers.*
> *For he today that sheds his blood with me*
> *Shall be my brother; be he ne'er so vile,*
> *This day shall gentle his condition. (Act IV, Sc. iii)*

Fighting at Agincourt with Harry "gentles" your "condition," it makes you into a gentleman; it gives you a new social identity. (It detracts little from the sentiment that the king is clearly engaging in hyperbole!) Because your honor attaches to you as a person of some specific social identity, we need to know what kind of person you are, before we can see what forms of honor are available to you.

Plainly, we may both gain and lose honor through the successes and failures of those with whom we share an identity. When the people of England hear of the victory at Agincourt, they can take pride in England's honor; when the French hear of their defeat, they will know and feel their country's shame. The pride I feel when my country's soldiers defend innocent civilians from men who are trying to massacre them in a country far away comes because I share in my nation's honor. As we shall see, there are analogous experiences for groups of many kinds: religions, classes, and families prominent among them. (Many cars here in America bear a sticker that says, "Proud Parent of an Honors Student.") Kang Youwei was moved, and equally aimed to move others, by a stake Chinese people shared in the honor of their country. In this chapter, then, I set out to examine a second revolution in the moral history of our species; this time, though, change was shaped not by alterations in the landscape of individual honor, but by transformations in ideas about the honor of a people.

THE BEGINNINGS OF THE GOLDEN LOTUS

The precise origins of footbinding are shrouded in controversy. There are traditions that associate its beginnings with the poet-king Li Yu, last of the Southern Tang rulers, who held out against Song rule until 975. (If this is right, then footbinding began nearly fifteen hundred years after the death of Confucius.) Howard Levy, author of one of the first modern histories of footbinding, records a reference in the work of a twelfth-century commentator to a text, now lost, which described Li Yu's "favored palace concubine," a woman known as "Lovely Maiden," "who was a slender-waisted beauty and a gifted dancer. He had a six-foot high lotus con-structed for her out of gold. . . . Lovely Maiden was ordered to bind her feet with white silk cloth to make the tips look like the points of a moon sickle. She then danced in the centre of the lotus, whirling about like a rising cloud."[12] Whatever the merits of the story as history, the bound foot of a Chinese woman came to be known as a golden lotus or lily.

Footbinding began as a sign of elevated status in an extremely hierarchical society. By the late thirteenth century, Levy writes, "families which claimed aristocratic lineage came to feel compelled to bind the feet of their girls . . . as a visible sign of upper-class distinction." The distinction was possible because women of the upper classes—aristocrats at the court or gentry in the provinces—did not need to work in the fields, as peasant women did, or take long walks to the market. In fact, their bound feet kept them from straying far from home, thus guaranteeing, as a fourteenth-century treatise put it (in an argument that was to be repeated many times over the centuries), their chastity.[13]

The golden lotus is connected from its beginnings with female honor. And, since honor was one of the essential prerequisites for respectable marriage—which was an arrangement between families, not the choice of individuals—Chinese women who expected to marry men of any social status needed to have their feet bound. Men came to long for small-footed women; and this painful practice was made bearable to women—as they endured it themselves, and as they witnessed the pain of daughters, nieces, and granddaughters—by the conviction that their tiny feet were simply beautiful.

This conviction is hard to share if you look at the pictures of the bare foot freed of its bindings that became a staple of later campaigners against the practice. But we have to remember that this was not what most people saw. For, once it was bound, a woman's foot was almost always covered in elegant, colorful, embroidered shoes.

In fact, one of the attributes of a Chinese woman of good family was skill in making and embroidering her own shoes, in colors appropriate for festival, for mourning, and for every day, as well as to wear at night. Sewing a set of shoes to take to one's husband's house was part of the preparation for marriage; and a woman's mother-in-law would judge her, in part, by the quality of the shoes she brought with her. Men would see their own wives' naked feet only in private. As the Englishwoman Mrs. Archibald Little, one of the great anti-footbinding campaigners, whom we shall be meeting again later, once put it: "Every Chinese, when he fondles the feet of his bride, likes to imagine that they are all that they appear—tiny, satin clad and beautifully embroidered."[14]

A woman would see her golden lotuses herself only when she took off the long binding strips to change them; washing her feet, powdering them with alum, re-binding them, and putting on her red sleeping shoes before retiring . . . or donning the elegant confections for daytime wear that others would glimpse beneath her skirt. But we should not assume that even the naked foot was the object of repugnance. Far from it. There are many photographs from the turn of the twentieth century of women proudly showing their golden lotuses; and admiration of these tiny broken feet, revealed in private without their bindings, is a regular theme of Chinese writing over the centuries.

THE CUSTOM SPREADS

Before the Manchus took over the empire, the imperial family was, of course, Chinese; and a Chinese emperor, at the apex of his society, had thousands of women reserved exclusively for his sexual use. The Forbidden City, where the emperor lived, was closed at night to all but the emperor, his eunuchs, his wives, and his concubines. The political scientist Gerry Mackie has suggested one reason why, in these circumstances, footbinding would have taken hold and spread.

The emperor, surrounded by all these women, will be concerned to make sure that the children they bear are his own offspring. The wives and concubines, on the other hand, most of whom, given their numbers, are unlikely to have any children at all, will have reason "to seek clandestine insemination from men more available" than the emperor. So there will be a constant struggle between the emperor, with his interest in ensuring their fidelity, and these women, who have reason to escape his control. The fact that all the males who worked in the inner heart of the palace were castrated was one reflection of this situation. But so, too, was the fact that the women's movements were limited through footbinding.

Mackie's key insight is that, once this system is in place, its influence will spread out from the palace.

> The next lower stratum, competing to provide wives and concubines to the apex, will imitate and exaggerate the fidelity-control practice so as to gain economic, social, and reproductive access to the palace. The vacuum of women in the first lower stratum will be filled by women moving up from the second lower stratum, who in turn will adopt the fidelity-control convention, and so on, all the way down.[15]

And so, in the course of the Mongol-led Yuan dynasty (1271–1368), footbinding spread southwards, at least among the elite. It increased in popularity among the upper classes of the Ming dynasty, as is evidenced in the great Ming dynasty erotic novel *Jin Ping Mei*, known in English as *The Golden Lotus* or *The Plum in the Golden Vase*, which appeared at the end of the sixteenth century. When Hsi-mên, a prosperous merchant, goes looking for a new wife, the go-between who is arranging the marriage finds an opportunity to lift the lady's skirt slightly, displaying her exquisite feet, three inches long and no wider than a thumb, very pointed and with high insteps. They were clad in a pair of scarlet shoes, embroidered in gold with a cloud design, with white silk high heels. Hsi-mên observed them with great satisfaction.[16]

The Manchus, who overthrew the Ming dynasty in 1644 and established the last of the imperial dynasties, the Qing (1644–1912), took a dim view of footbinding, however, and they tried from time to time, with varying degrees of enthusiasm, to eradicate the golden lotus.

Their first decrees abolishing footbinding were issued immediately after their arrival. But far from declining under their rule, it spread further among the Chinese population. Even some Manchu aristocrats ignored official proscription of the practice, and decrees against it were rescinded when they proved ineffective. There are reports of footbinding in the nineteenth century among some of the minorities who lived in the empire: Jews in Hunan, some Muslims outside Gansu Province. Most Mongols and Tibetans abstained, as did the Hakka of southern China. By and large, the practice was much less common among the poor, especially in the south, in areas of intensive agriculture, where women had a part to play in the rice fields. But there are accounts that suggest that even some beggars and water carriers had bound feet in urban Hunan, as well as in many rural areas in the north.[17]

By the late nineteenth century, then, Chinese women, especially those of the upper classes, had been binding the feet of their daughters for nearly a millennium, though the practice had also been banned, off and on, by imperial decree for more than two centuries. Women with natural feet were mocked; women with small feet, especially those with the smallest golden lotuses, less than three inches long, were praised and prized, and their feet were the objects of erotic attention. Chinese novels and erotic manuals spoke of men who were aroused by the shuffling gait of the footbound woman or excited by stroking the unwrapped bound foot. They describe sexual positions in which men could fondle the unwrapped feet of their lovers. There were public tiny-foot contests, in which appreciative audiences were able to comment on and evaluate the "diminutive sizes and proportioned shapes" of the silk-wrapped golden lotuses.[18]

THE PAIN OF BINDING

Footbinding was done to girls, some of them as young as three or four years old. If it was done with the aim of making as small a golden lotus as possible, it was intensely painful. The binding crushed the four smaller toes under the sole and compressed the rear of the anklebone toward the sole too, forcing the bones of the foot into an arch much higher than anything that occurs naturally, and creating a sort of cleft. Often bound feet had to be cleansed of blood and pus; occasionally they putrefied and toes dropped off. Eventually—after months and years—the pain diminished, presumably because the sensory nerves were permanently damaged, but walking was usually difficult for women with bound feet. Missionary doctors in the late nineteenth century—who were grinding, no doubt, a somewhat ethnocentric ax—reported cases where the binding caused ulceration, gangrene, loss of one or both feet, even, in the worst case, death.[19]

It is clear that the ideal length of the three-inch lotus was rarely achieved, especially outside the upper classes. Peasants and laborers often underwent a looser form of binding, which might begin when the girl was older; and this process was both less hobbling and less painful. The husband of one elderly woman whose feet had been bound insisted that the less deformed five-inch feet of some ordinary workingwomen were no obstacle to walking or carrying heavy loads. A three-inch foot, on the other hand, did not allow you to walk long distances. Women with the three-inch lotus were often carried about in sedan chairs and often supported by servants when they walked. Most women with bound feet, however, did not need such assistance.[20]

Since the bindings were worn both day and night, the bound foot had a distinctive odor—one that some found extremely unpleasant and others, notoriously, found sexually exciting. The pseudonymous eighteenth-century footbinding enthusiast who called himself the "Doctor of the Fragrant Lotus" produced a monograph entitled *A Golden Garden Miscellany*, which consisted of unconnected observations about footbinding, among which was this gem:

> *Unbearable*—painful corns; smelling the awful odor when the binding is suddenly removed.[87]

There is no doubt, then, that everyone understood not only that footbinding could limit movement and help keep women subject to their families and to men, but also that it was extremely painful.

Almost as soon as it began, there were literati who opposed

it. During the Song dynasty (960–1279), a writer is recorded as having said: "Children not yet four or five years old, innocent and without crime, are caused to suffer limitless pain." And a traditional proverb runs: "One pair of tiny feet, but two cisterns of tears." Even those who favored the practice admitted it caused girls pain; two of the Doctor of the Fragrant Lotus's other apothegms were these:

> *Slight displeasure*—the mother who loves her daughters but still has to bind their feet.
> *Can't bear to hear*—the cries of a young girl as her feet are bound for the first time.[22]

As with dueling, what brought footbinding to an end cannot have been the discovery of arguments against it. The arguments are obvious: and they were widely known from the earliest days of the golden lotus.

THE LAST DAYS OF EMPIRE

To understand the end of footbinding at the turn of the twentieth century, one needs to see this change in the context of the many changes that took place in China in the latter nineteenth century, as the Qing dynasty fell into its final decline. The Qing was a Manchu dynasty, and it began when the well-organized Manchurian state, created in the early seventeenth century by the Khan Nurhaci, finally achieved its long-held aim of conquering the Middle Kingdom. Once they had restored order—overcoming the bandits who had plagued the north and defeating the rebel Li

Zicheng, who had sacked Beijing—the Manchus extended their control throughout the empire.

Though they had conquered the empire, they nevertheless maintained the structure of Chinese government: in particular, they kept the system of civil service exams that created and sustained the class of literati trained in the Confucian classics.[23] The Qianlong Emperor—who ruled China from 1736 to 1799—committed more than 350 scholars and nearly 4,000 copyists working from 1773 to 1798 to cataloguing Chinese literary culture in the 2.3 million pages of the *Siku quanshu,* "The Complete book of the four imperial repositories" (though he also ordered the suppression of several thousand volumes identified in this exercise that he deemed in various respects objectionable). One of the key court appointments was the Manchu emperor's tutor, whose job, among other things, was to guide the emperor in his study of Chinese philosophical traditions.

The most successful of the literati were those who passed the exams, earning titles, honor for their families, exemption from labor service, and the right to wear distinctive clothing.[24] Over the centuries, retired literati, returning home, created a local gentry diffused across the empire.[25] The gentry saw knowledge of the classics, skill in poetry and essay writing, calligraphy and painting, as attributes of the men of their class. If the sword defined the English gentleman in the eighteenth century, here was a gentry whose ideal for millennia was the pen—or rather, the calligraphy brush. In the eighteenth century, an English gentleman lived much of his time in the country and served his king above all else in wartime; a Chinese gentleman's ideal was to live in town and serve the emperor in government, whether locally or in the imperial or provincial capital.

Qing society became increasingly culturally conservative and puritanical. In part this was a response to a conviction that the collapse of the Ming dynasty had been a result of a failure to adhere strictly to Confucian notions of duty and a consequent general moral decline. The escalating adherence to rigorously conceived Confucian ideals showed itself in a variety of ways. Through the eighteenth century and into the nineteenth, for example, widows of the upper classes increasingly refused to remarry: the construction of memorial arches to faithful widows "got so out of hand," as the historian Patricia Ebrey has put it, "that in 1827 the government decreed that only collective arches could be built and in 1843 that only widows who had gone to the extreme of committing suicide should be honored by arches."[26]

This conservatism combined with the strengthening of the central government to produce a society that was stable and technologically advanced by global standards, but extremely hierarchical and authoritarian. And while the three Qing emperors from 1662 to 1795 expanded their empire and secured control of their state, the world around them was beginning to close in. The Chinese had traded for centuries with Japan and Europe's major maritime empires—Portuguese, Dutch, and British. But they had regarded these foreigners as evidently inferior. In 1793, the Qianlong Emperor, accepting the ideology of his Han Chinese subjects, responded to a diplomatic overture from Britain as if it were simply another offer of tribute from one of the many admiring second rank nations:

> You, O King, live beyond the confines of many seas, nevertheless, impelled by your humble desire to partake of the benefits

of our civilization, you have dispatched a mission respectfully
bearing your memorial. . . . To show your devotion, you have
also sent offerings of your country's produce.

Though he was gracious enough to accept George III's "offerings,"
the emperor felt the need to point out that this was only because
he recognized the spirit in which they had been presented: "As
your Ambassador can see for himself, we possess all things. I set no
value on objects, strange or ingenious, and have no use for your
country's manufactures."[27] Feigned or not, the misunderstanding
is comical.

Half a century later, Britain, with its new military and shipping
technologies, was in a position to threaten China from a capital
half a world away; and the United States was using new steamships
loaded with firepower to flex its muscle in the Pacific. In 1854,
Commodore Perry forced the Japanese to end more than two centuries of self-imposed isolation. A few decades further on, with
the Meiji Restoration, Japan itself was a major modern economic
and military power. Industrialization was changing the world and
China's failure to keep pace increasingly undermined its relative
position.

China's first significant notice of the troubles that modernizing
foreigners could pose came with the first Opium War at the turn
of the 1840s. British commercial interests had developed a profitable business growing opium in India and selling it to China.
In the late eighteenth century, the British East India Company,
which produced the drug in Bengal, had massively increased the
supplies in China, against the wishes of the emperor, by arranging an elaborate system of smuggling; they needed something to

offer the Chinese to pay for the tea that they were turning into England's stimulant of choice. In 1839, the Qing rulers decided that opium was simply too harmful both to its people and to its exchequer—hundreds of thousands of kilograms of silver were flowing out annually in the opium trade—to allow it to continue. The emperor sent an experienced senior official, named Lin Zexu, to the port of Guangzhou, the only city where Europeans were permitted to live and do business, to insist, after decades of failure, on the end of the importation of opium.

In May 1839, the British Chief Superintendent of Trade, Charles Elliot, was forced to hand over British opium stocks for destruction. Two months later, rioting British sailors destroyed a temple and murdered a Chinese man down the coast in Kowloon. When the Chinese authorities asked for the sailors to be handed over for trial, Elliot declined. The Chinese then insisted that the British agree not only to cease trading in opium but also to recognize the authority of Chinese courts. Rather than submit to these demands, Chief Superintendent Elliot ordered the British to leave Guangzhou and cease trading with the Chinese altogether.

In the summer of 1840 a large flotilla of British ships set out from Singapore, with the aim of reestablishing British trade into China on the earlier terms by force of arms. Along with four gunboats powered by steam, there were more than forty other ships, carrying, among them, some four thousand British and Indian marines. They did not impress Lin, who reported their arrival, when they anchored in June off the port of Macao. They seemed to be engaged in trading opium, he told the emperor, and were otherwise not likely to cause too much trouble. "That is all they are doing, and as Your Majesty knows, there is really nothing they can do."[28]

He could not have been more massively mistaken. Two years and several naval battles later, the British had seized Shanghai, and surrounded Nanjing. The Chinese surrendered. At the Treaty of Nanjing, the Chinese were forced to agree to humiliating terms. They had to pay huge indemnities of silver, to open five "treaty ports," to lower trade tariffs, to cede Hong Kong, and to agree that all British subjects in China were to be governed by British law. They also guaranteed Britain "most favored nation status," which meant that any concessions won by other powers must also be granted to them.

In the decades that followed, Europeans made further impositions on the terms of trade, including forcing the opening of further ports and a renewed opium trade. They achieved these aims by establishing military supremacy on land and sea. And, in 1846, in a move that was to have considerable consequences for the issue of footbinding, the French government insisted that Christian missions be permitted to enter all of China.[29]

The punitive terms of the Treaty of Nanjing and the seemingly endless series of concessions made under force of arms in the decades that followed—up to the Treaty of Shimonoseki that was to exercise Kang Youwei and his confreres more than half a century later—diminished the authority of the Manchu emperors. Things were made worse by a series of internal revolts culminating in the Taiping Rebellion of 1850–54, which was led by Hong Xiuquan, a Hakka from a farming family in Guangdong, who was educated enough to take (though not to pass) the imperial exams. (The Hakka are a southern ethnic group of Han Chinese.)

Hong had come into contact with Christianity, and he declared, after he had a vision of a middle-aged white man, that he was Jesus Christ's younger brother. He called the earthly kingdom he proclaimed, with its capital in Nanjing, "*Tai Ping Tian Guo*—the Heavenly Kingdom of Great Peace"—which is where we get our name for the rebellion. But the Chinese authorities referred to the Taipings as the Long-Haired Bandits, because they wore their hair in the old Chinese manner and not in the queue, the ponytail that the Manchus had imposed on the Han Chinese.

Hong learned Christian practices from a missionary and took to prayer and hymn singing, adopting at the same time a particularly puritan regime of hostility to alcohol, opium, and prostitution, and insisting on the end of Chinese traditions, including ancestral shrines and temples (which he thought idolatrous), and, to return to the matter in hand, footbinding. Hong combined his opposition to these Chinese traditions with virulently anti-Manchu feelings. When the Taiping forces took Nanjing in 1853, they killed every Manchu man woman and child they captured, giving many of them deaths of horrifying brutality.

Hong's hostility to footbinding anticipated the campaigns of later more orthodox Christian missions from Europe and the United States. It is possible that he was simply expressing traditional Hakka hostility to the practice.[30] Since the Taiping rebels had a vision of equality between men and women—which was not a major theme of Christian evangelism—it is also hard to know how much of his opposition to footbinding was, in his mind, a matter of Christian morality, and how much was a consequence of a certain proto-feminism. As I noted earlier, the notion that footbinding helped keep women "in their place" was a commonplace in China centuries before 1850.

Certainly, Hong was so wildly heretical—his initial visions

were of Jesus commanding him to destroy demons—that the European Christians who were now firmly established in coastal cities, such as Shanghai, did not regard him as an ally. When the Taiping rebels approached Shanghai in the early 1860s, they were firmly repulsed by European forces. Eventually, a Confucian literatus from Hunan named Zeng Guofan—who, like many Han Chinese, was appalled by Hong's defections from Confucianism—organized a huge new army of over 100,000 soldiers to defeat the rebels. By the time Zeng defeated the Taipings, Hong had died; but many others had taken notice of the weaknesses the Taiping revolt had revealed. Zeng had to keep his army moving to defeat insurrections elsewhere.

Beset by losses to foreigners and shaken by insurgent threats to the government, some in Beijing drew the conclusion that they must learn from the rest of the world. They formed what they called a "Self-Strengthening Movement," led by figures at court like the Manchu prince Yixin. These policies were carried out at the provincial level by men like Zeng Guofan and his students. Zeng himself was rewarded with greater authority after his success in defeating the Taiping revolt.[31] His younger colleague Li Hongzhang wrote to Beijing in 1864, explaining that China faced "the greatest crisis since its unification under the First Emperor in 221 BC."[32] Li's solution was that China should begin to borrow Western technology and train its own people to make and to use it. The government allowed newspapers, created a translators' school, built dockyards and factories, coal mines and cotton mills, and ordered modern weapons and ships. It built the first railroads and telegraphs, and opened Chinese embassies in the major capitals of the world, from Tokyo to Washington.

Chinese men and women began to study abroad in Japan and even in Europe and the United States. But the empress dowager never sided fully with those who favored these changes; instead, she played them off against Confucian traditionalists. The arguments of the Self-Strengtheners were resisted by many of the literati who were not taken in by the Chinese-sounding slogan of "Self-Strengthening"; they saw that it meant adopting the modernization by Westernization that the Japanese were undergoing. Like a multitude of Bartlebys, they preferred not to.

Not only did they dislike the local modernizers, they regarded the foreign Christians as a threat to their own status as the intellectual voice of their civilization. The persistent opposition of Protestant missionaries, especially women, to the practice of footbinding was one among many points of contention.

THE RESPONSE OF THE LITERATI

There had been Christians in China before: notably Matteo Ricci (who arrived in 1582) and his fellow Jesuits. But it had been China's decision to admit them. They had been dressed in the Chinese manner and, if they lived in Beijing, it was on condition that they would never return home. The later nineteenth century was the first time Christian evangelism was permitted almost total free rein. Catholic and Protestant missions from Europe and from North America built churches and schools and converted some Chinese—especially, as had happened over and over again in the history of Christian missions, among the poor. Unlike the Catholics, the Protestants sent both men and women to do this work; and the women missionaries, striding confidently about on their large feet, made it their special vocation to educate and uplift the women.

A generation ago, a Columbia graduate student, Virginia Chau, showed that there were stirrings against footbinding among the literati before the arrival of the Christians. Chau has identified a seventeenth-century Ming poet who delighted in the large fleshy toes of Manchu women. In the later eighteenth century, the poet and artist Yuan Mei—who admired women's poetry and took women as students—wrote, in a letter to a friend who had expressed a desire for a lotus-footed concubine, that in following the taste of Li Yu (whose concubine, Lovely Maiden, you will recall, was one mythical source of the idea of the golden lotus) he was copying an unbefitting model, "the last king of a conquered kingdom."[33] His younger contemporary, the poet Qian Yong, pointed out (in the spirit of Confucian classicism that led to those many widows' memorials) that footbinding was not mentioned in the classics, and argued that there was a historical correlation between the spread of footbinding and the weakening of kingdoms. Qian Yong went on—in a line of reasoning that would have been recognized by Francis Bacon—to argue that, since footbinding had been adopted by the lower classes, the gentry should avoid it.[34]

Chau also points to Li Ruzhen, whose novel *Flowers in the Mirror* (published in 1828, but probably begun some two decades earlier) is a sort of Chinese *Gulliver's Travels*. Li expressed his sympathy for the situation of women in general in a satire about a Woman's Kingdom, which describes sympathetically the sufferings of Merchant Lin, who is chosen to be a concubine of the female "King" and is subjected to the pain and indignities of footbinding. After days of pain, Merchant Lin tears off his "embroidered shoes and silk bandages. 'Go tell your "King" to put me to death at once, or let my feet loose' . . . ," he says.[35]

But despite these early critics, the organized resistance begins only after the intrusions of the missionaries. Christian schools for girls began to be opened in the 1860s in many parts of the country. In Hangzhou, in the Yangtze River delta, the Church Mission opened a school for girls in 1867, which required "from the first," as Mrs. Archibald Little wrote, "that the feet of the girls should be unbound, and that they should not be compelled to marry against their own consent. . . ." Similarly, when the Methodists opened a girls' school in Beijing, they required all the girls to have their feet unbound.[36]

In 1874, the Reverend John Macgowan of the London Mission Society, who had been campaigning for some fifteen years against footbinding, along with his wife, called a meeting of Christian women in Xiamen (then known in English as Amoy) along the coast from Zhangzhou, in Fujian Province. "At the end of the meeting, nine women 'signed' a pledge to eradicate the heathen practice in their homes and beyond by drawing a cross against their names written out by a Chinese pastor."[37] Eventually other, mostly working-class women joined up, pledging not to bind the feet of their daughters and undergoing the often painful process of unbinding themselves.[38] But progress was slow. For decades the Macgowans went about their work recruiting to their "Quit-Footbinding Society," echoing the name of the "Quit-Opium Smoking" societies that anticipated by more than a century the anti-addiction work of Alcoholics Anonymous.[39] This was the first Anti-Footbinding Society in China.

The movement found support, from the 1880s on, among increasing numbers of young Chinese men and women who had returned from study abroad. They included young women from the gentry and the prosperous merchant classes, who had been sent to Japan, and who came back committed to educating a new generation of Chinese girls both physically and mentally for a more emancipated world. These were China's first feminists, committed to women's equality. The schools they started put physical education—sports and exercise—at the heart of the curriculum. Their practice presupposed that women's feet should not be bound.[40]

The missionaries, for their part, increasingly took pains to address the literati. They set up newspapers and magazines, including *Wanguo gongbao* (*The Review of the Times*), founded in 1868 by Reverend Young John Allen of the American Southern Methodist Episcopal Mission and edited by him until his death in 1907. *The Review of the Times* gave the literati access—in classical Chinese—to ideas and events from the world outside China, allowing them to see new options for dealing with the crisis in their society. Equally influential was the work of Reverend Timothy Richard of the Baptist Missionary Society, who edited *Shi bao* (*The Eastern Times*) in Tianjin for a period beginning in 1890, at the invitation of the distinguished literatus Li Hongzhang.[41]

Richard grasped better than most Protestant missionaries that the key to China lay with the literati. He dressed as they did; spent a great deal of time, energy, and money writing, translating, and publishing Christian literature—catechisms, sermons, the New Testament—and preparing himself by studying the texts that formed the core of the training for the national examinations. Horrified by the famine he witnessed in Shandong and Shanxi in the 1870s and by the inability of the Manchu regime and its mandarin agents in the provinces to respond to it, Richard concluded that what China needed above all was the knowledge of modern science that was—with Christianity—one of Western civilization's greatest fruits. "In pondering Western civilization," he wrote,

> I felt that its advantage over Chinese civilization was due to the fact that it sought to discover the workings of God in Nature, and to apply the laws of Nature for the service of mankind. . . . I was convinced that if I could lecture the officials and scholars and interest them in these miracles of science, I would be able to point out to them ways in which they could utilize the forces of God in Nature for the benefit of their fellow countrymen. In this way I could influence them to build railways, to open mines, to avert recurrences of famine, and save the people from their grinding poverty.[42]

It was this modernizing Christianity, with its vision of science and technology in the service of human needs, that the modernizing literati responded to. Kang Youwei—the *jinshi* who wrote the memorial against footbinding with which we began—once declared: "I owe my conversion to reform and my knowledge of reform chiefly to the writings of two missionaries, Rev. Timothy Richard . . . and the Rev. Dr. Allen. . . ."[43] But—we should be clear—it was reform to which he was converted, not Christianity.

Indeed, the one area where Christian missionaries made rather little headway was in the task of actually creating Christians. "By 1894," John King Fairchild and Merel Goldman write, "the Protestant mission effort supported over 1,300 missionaries, mainly

British, American, and Canadian, and maintained some 500 stations—each with a church, residences, street chapels, usually a small school, and possibly a hospital or dispensary—in about 350 different cities and towns." And yet, in this country of more than 400 million people, there were not yet 60,000 Chinese converts.[44] The good news the missionaries brought, for many sympathetic Chinese, was Western modernity, not salvation through Christ.

Certainly, the Westernizing newspapers and journals opened members of the literati, like Kang, to a more cosmopolitan vision; and it was from among their readers that a second kind of anti-footbinding society developed. Kang wrote in his autobiography that it was *The Review of the Times* that introduced him to Western ideas, beginning in 1883, and that this was what led him to start thinking about footbinding.[45] He had, he said, been distressed by the pain his sisters underwent when their feet were bound. When the time came, he declined to allow the binding of his own daughter's feet. His family urged him to change his mind. Instead, he started an Unbound Foot Association—the *Bu Guozu Hui*—in Guangzhou in 1894, with another member of the literati, who had traveled to America and who, like Kang, was not willing to have his daughter's feet bound. Later he moved his base of operations to Shanghai and it eventually had more than 10,000 members.[46] And then, in 1898, he made the written appeal to the emperor with which we began: the plea to end footbinding once and for all.

Macgowan represented the missionary program, Kang represented the new reforming literati. In the final development of the Natural Foot movement, there was one other important voice: that of elite expatriate women, the prosperous wives of the businessmen and officials of the commercial ports on the coast. In the

1890s, Macgowan met Mrs. Archibald Little in Shanghai. Inspired by him, she gathered the expatriate elite in Shanghai, summoned Macgowan to speak, and founded a new national anti-footbinding society, the *Tianzu Hui*, which Mrs. Little translated as "Natural Foot Society." (Reverend Macgowan preferred to render *Tianzu Hui* as "Heavenly Foot Society," emphasizing, no doubt, the religious significance of abandoning un-Christian traditions.)[47] Timothy Richard helped them by producing and publishing their anti-footbinding pamphlets.

Mrs. Little had come to China in 1887, after marrying Archibald Little, an Englishman who had arrived in the Orient nearly thirty years earlier, and was, by the time of their marriage, a successful businessman, based in Chongqing, in Sichuan. She had already had a successful career under her maiden name—Alicia Bewicke—as the author of satirical novels about the empty social lives of the rich and the follies of the marriage market.[48] So she had had an independent life as a young woman and she conducted, with her husband's support, an active campaign against footbinding all over China.

Perhaps because she was not a missionary, Mrs. Little grasped that the association of anti-footbinding with Christianity in this overwhelmingly Confucian society was a handicap. Her tours through the country were addressed to the literati as much as anyone. In 1900 she succeeded in converting Li Hongzhang, by then Governor-General of Guangzhou, to her cause.

But other leading members of the literati found their way to the same conclusion. In 1897, Zhang Zhidong, Governor-General of Hunan and Hubei, published an essay supporting the campaign against footbinding, which became one of the most powerful weapons in the arsenal of the Natural Foot Society.[49] At one of Mrs. Little's meetings in Hubei's capital, Wuhan, where she had decorated the hall with "huge placards" in Zhang's "inimitable" literary style, "one military mandarin only deigned to study this placard without condescending apparently to listen to any of my words of wisdom, but he signed on as a member of our society at the end. . . ."[50] The leadership of the *Tianzu Hui* was transferred into Chinese hands when Mrs. Little left for England with her ailing husband in 1907.[51] Soon after, it faded away—not because its cause lost support but because, at least among the upper classes, its arguments had prevailed.

In dealing with the problems facing their society at the end of the nineteenth century, China's modernizing intellectuals, like those who resisted them, were guided by a profound loyalty to their nation and to its deepest intellectual traditions. Many of the modernizers insisted on the distinction between *ti* (substance) and *yong* (application); they believed, as they said, in "Chinese learning for fundamental principles, Western learning for the practical applications."[52] In attacking footbinding, they pointed out that it was a practice that was unknown in the time of Confucius, and, indeed, for much more than a millennium after his death. But some also said that the arguments and publications of the missionaries and the *Tianzu Hui* had had a profound impact on their thinking—in no small part by revealing how much footbinding had incurred disrespect for China and its civilization.

HONOR WORLDS

I said earlier that honor inhabits an honor world: a group of people who acknowledge the same codes, and whose respect is sought. It's important to understand, though, that an honor world need not be limited to one's own society. Henry V certainly believes he deserves the respect of foreign princes. Your honor world consists of people who understand and acknowledge the code of honor, even if, like English peasants, the code does not demand much (if anything) of them. The honor world of Chinese intellectuals at the start of the nineteenth century didn't include people elsewhere; but Kang's memorial shows that by the end of the century, some of them, at least, saw themselves as part of a wider world of nations, engaged in the assessment of each other's societies. Now their honor world included the Japanese, Europeans, and Americans whose critical evaluations undermined China's claim to respect.

In an honor world, some people are defined as your honor peers, because the codes make the same demands of you as of them. For Prince Hal, so far as his military honor goes, his honor peers are gentlemen . . . and not just English gentlemen, all gentlemen. English ladies are the honor peers of ladies generally, even though they are governed by very different rules. Because people do not necessarily recognize that an honor code is the product of a particular society and a particular place, they can mistakenly suppose someone to be their honor peer, who isn't. And your honor world consists of more than your honor peers: many codes of honor, as we have seen, make different demands on women, as opposed to men (as is often the case with chastity), but both women and men belong to the honor world of those codes. One of the ways the missionaries achieved their influence was by stressing that they regarded the literati as part of their own honor world. People like Reverend Richard, who so clearly respected much in the Confucian heritage and who chose to dress, himself, like a Chinese scholar, encouraged the thought that Westerners and Chinese could not only appeal to the same standards but might even be honor peers.

THE BOXER REBELLION AND ITS AFTERMATH

Those hundred days of reform in 1898 that gave Kang his extraordinary moment of influence ended as abruptly as they began. The radical changes the emperor proposed alienated the bureaucracy in the palace and the capital. The old exams had created them; the new science was exactly what they did not know; they did not care to be abolished. The conservatives waited until they had the support of the empress dowager and then, essentially, staged a coup. Kang was lucky to escape to Japan; six other reform leaders, including Kang's brother, were executed. The empress dowager returned to the center of power, sitting "behind the curtain" even when the emperor was in view.[53] As a result she was in charge when the last great upheaval of the Qing dynasty—the Boxer Rebellion—began in the long, hot summer of 1900.[54]

The Boxers (as members of the Society of Righteous and Harmonious Fists came to be known in the West) believed that many of the problems their society faced were the result of the unnatural presence of foreigners in their country. The foreign presence interfered with the proper flow of energy; disturbed the harmony between human settlement and nature—the *feng shui*—with their railroads and telegraph wires; upset the ancestors. The Boxers apparently had the support of one faction in the palace, the conservative Manchu Iron Hats, who thought they could use the movement to rid the country of the pernicious influence of foreigners once and for all. But another faction, based in the Zongli Yamen, which was in charge of foreign relations, seems to have recognized that provoking the European powers and Japan would prove to be extremely unwise. The faction that knew the foreigners best proved to be right. When the Western nations sent in forces to reestablish order in Beijing, they easily overran its Chinese defenders and plundered the palace and the city.

Li Hongzhang—he of the Self-Strengthening Movement—negotiated a settlement. The terms of the agreement were as punitive as any that had been imposed in the long sequence of unsuccessful wars with the West. But Cixi was left in place. The Qing dynasty had another decade to totter on.[55]

By 1902, the empress dowager herself issued an anti-footbinding edict, which focused on the fact that the practice was unhealthy; but she urged, rather than commanded, its discontinuance. The empress "commended" the "gentry and notables of Chinese descent" to "earnestly exhort their families and all who come under their influence to abstain henceforth from that evil practice and by these means gradually abolish the custom forever." She had "carefully avoided the words 'we prohibit,' " she continued, "so that dishonest officials and . . . underlings may not have any excuse to brow beat and oppress her Chinese subjects. . . ."[56] This was hardly a ringing call to abolition, but it was a beginning; and it reflected the pressure on the throne from the foreigners who were now even more firmly ensconced in her dominion. On November 14, 1908, the emperor died; the dowager empress died less than a day later. The last emperor was not yet three; by the time he was seven, in February 1912, he had abdicated as Emperor of China.

As the dynasty came to an end, the new republic—led by

modernizers, many of whom had been educated in the West or in Japan—spoke out more forcefully. In March 1911, Sun Yatsen issued an order banning footbinding as a cruel and destructive custom.[57] It was one of the many symbols of the old imperial world—like the pigtail—that the new republican order would replace. Aside from the short-lived conservative presidency of Yuan Shikai, who sought to reinstitute Confucianism as a national philosophy, China's subsequent governors—both Communist and Nationalist—were modernizers who opposed footbinding, advocated women's equality, and encouraged women to engage in sports and develop their bodies.[58] But the China they inherited had already lost its faith in footbinding.

THE PLACE OF HONOR

The anti-footbinding associations had roots, as we have seen, among Christian missionaries and the Western business elite, but also among those members of the literati, like Kang, who saw some degree of Westernization as necessary if China was to find its place in the modern world. The focus of the literati was on the good of China, first: if ending footbinding was good for women so much the better, no doubt. So their writings have a nationalist flavor. Some of their arguments were instrumental: they insisted, for example, that the havoc wrought in military invasions from abroad was made worse by the fact that so many women were literally unable to run away; and they argued that the physical vigor of women who could engage in sports because their feet were free would make them mothers of healthier children. But they insisted regularly, too, that footbinding needed to end because it was a source of national shame. In his footbinding memorial, as we saw, Kang had made this central to his argument.

Indeed, the memorial, as Virginia Chau reports, starts with the claim that it is "a shame for China to have such a barbarous custom, which makes it a laughingstock in the eyes of foreigners," and ends with this closing peroration:

> speaking of the law of the country, it is a most unjustifiable penalty; speaking of the maintenance of harmony in the family, it harms the love of parents for their children; speaking of the strengthening of the army, it leaves generation after generation of weak descendants; and finally, speaking of beauty and customs, it becomes a subject of ridicule to foreigners. It is therefore intolerable.[59]

Kang begins and ends with the nation's honor—or rather, with his country's shame. His protégé Liang Qichao, another of the leading Chinese intellectuals of the early twentieth century, wrote in 1896: "It seems that this ridiculous custom has flourished generation after generation against imperial prohibition and become the laughingstock of foreigners."[60]

The concern for the nation's honor persisted well into the new century, long after the practice had gone into a serious decline. One writer in the 1930s asked if it was not better to allow the practice to die out gradually—with the poor following the example of the rich, as they had as the practice was established: "Why disturb the peace and interfere? If we say that binding must be eradicated because foreigners ridicule us for doing this, it must be admitted that they ridicule us for other reasons as well." Footbinding followed the

Chinese as they traveled the world. Levy recounts the story of a Chinese woman, who made a living on the streets of Paris in the middle of the 1930s, charging people to look at her golden lotuses. "Overseas Chinese in Paris," he writes, "became indignant and protested to the Chinese Consulate that her behavior was an affront to national honor." The Japanese scholar Gotō Asaro, writing in 1939, summarized the situation succinctly: anti-footbinding, he said, had been aimed at "saving China's 'National Face.'"[61]

ACTING TOGETHER

Most modern people will take it for granted that someone could be motivated by a concern for their nation's honor, so the story I've been telling in this chapter will probably strike you as easy enough to grasp. But there is, when you think about it, something slightly odd about the underlying idea. In the case of the individual, we can see how honor makes sense. Each of us cares to be worthy of respect. Merited respect is intrinsically valuable, and also usually reflects judgments about how well you are doing by your own standards. (It is shared standards, after all, that bind an honor world together.) So, in the individual case, the honor paid to you by others gives you reason to suppose that you are living up to your own ideals. But why should *my* worth be tied up with the worth of things done in the name of my nation? It is a fact that people esteem us if we belong to estimable social groups and disrespect us when we belong to disreputable ones. But shouldn't we ask them why? When someone acts well on behalf of my country, it's hard to see how I—as opposed to my praiseworthy fellow countryman—have merited respect.

One response to this puzzle would be to deny that what we feel when our nation merits disrespect is, in fact, real shame. Maybe what we feel is more like what happens when someone you care about is caught doing something unworthy; you don't feel shame yourself, you feel shame, so to speak, for them. And just as we might wince when we see a friend slice his hand while chopping onions, so we may blush for him when he acts dishonorably.

This form of sympathy—in its strict etymological sense of feeling *with* another—certainly explains some occasions where we have feelings that are not, strictly speaking, warranted, or, in any case, not warranted in the standard way. But it is not a plausible explanation in the case of national pride and shame, because there isn't usually a person to respond to sympathetically in this way at all. Whose individual shame am I vicariously sharing when the Congress passes a foolish resolution? I don't know which members of Congress voted for it and I may know that mine, with whom I am most likely to feel sympathy, voted against it. But even when there is someone we might be identifying with—when we feel shame at an atrocity carried our by members of our armed forces, say—we can distinguish between a sympathetic blush for the men who did it and a sense of national shame; not least because, if they have betrayed us, we may not feel sympathy for these men at all.

I think there is a better way to understand national honor. It begins with an elementary observation: many of the groups to which we belong do things collectively. Sometimes, for example, and not just in democracies, it makes sense to say that the nation acts. When a country goes to war or imposes a trade embargo or sends humanitarian aid or supports a resolution in the Security

Council, this is something that its citizens do not individually but together. The act is done in their name, but it is often their act in deeper ways than this. The individuals who act in the nation's name are shaped by a culture they have created together, under command of a government elected by its citizens; they are responding to values transmitted and sustained by a civil society that is made up of that nation's citizens. When it makes sense to speak of our country's aims and the picture of the world that guides the pursuit of them, it makes sense, too, to speak of what the nation does as something we, the people, do together.

Whether we should understand talk of the actions of collective agents as literal or metaphorical, and which kinds of collective agents it makes sense to speak of in this way, have both been subjects of lively debate in recent philosophy. I do not want, here, to take a stand on these issues. I want only to begin by insisting that we *do* talk this way; and that, absent a persuasive argument against doing so, we have the argument of custom for continuing.

But we have a better argument. In J. M. Coetzee's recent novel *A Diary of a Bad Year*, the protagonist writes—in one of his essays, reproduced in the text—of his response to a report in *The New Yorker* magazine that the U.S. administration has sanctioned torture and subverted conventions proscribing it:

Demosthenes: Whereas the slave fears only pain, what the free man fears most is shame. If we grant the truth of what the *New Yorker* claims, then the issue for individual Americans becomes a moral one: how, in the face of this shame to which I am subjected, do I behave? How do I save my honor?

Here is a reminder of why the sentiment of national honor may be worth preserving. Like individual honor, it can motivate us together to see if, together, we can do what is right. Though the issue is moral, what engages each American is not just morality but also honor. Just as in Wellington's duel honesty was at issue but honor produced the motivations, so in Kang Youwei's campaign, the suffering of girls and young women was at issue but honor drove him forward. Coetzee's narrator rightly emphasizes the fact that we may have as little choice in these collective feelings as we do in caring for our individual esteem.

He reflects on his response to a stirring performance of Sibelius's Fifth Symphony: the "large, swelling emotion" that the composer had meant his hearers to feel.

> What would it have been like, I wondered, to be a Finn in the audience at the first performance of the symphony in Helsinki nearly a century ago, and feel that swell overtake one? The answer: one would have felt proud, proud that one of us could put together such sounds, proud that out of nothing we human beings can make such stuff. Contrast with that one's feelings of shame that we, our people, have made Guantanamo. Musical creation on the one hand, a machine for inflicting pain and humiliation on the other: the best and the worst that human beings are capable of.[62]

The honor world addressed by people who feel pride or shame in what their nation or their fellow nationals are doing is the whole human world. To feel these sentiments you must have what the American Declaration of Independence called, in one of Thomas

Jefferson's many elegant formulations, "a decent respect to the opinions of mankind." Kang Youwei's concern for his people's reputation required him to think of outsiders as people whose respect mattered; he did not have the contempt for barbarians that had for so long been his culture's basic attitude to the world beyond its borders (the attitude, you will recall, of the Qianlong Emperor's response to the embassy of George III). This sense of one's own country as an actor in a wider world of other nations is one of the central psychological underpinnings of modern nationalism.[63] And it is why the nation's honor can be mobilized to motivate its citizens.

Part of what spurs us to do what our country needs us to do is a pride in country that depends on our thinking "we" have done great things. It depends, that is, on a sense that we are entitled to national esteem: that we are, in fact, an honorable nation. Ernest Renan—great French historian and nationalist—caught this spirit in 1882 in his indispensable essay "What Is a Nation?" when he wrote:

> The nation, like the individual, is the culmination of a long past of efforts, sacrifices and acts of devotion. The cult of ancestors is the most legitimate of all: the ancestors made us what we are. An heroic past, great men, glory—I mean real glory—this is the social capital on which the national idea is based.[64]

Patriotism is sometimes criticized as a form of idolatry. And because it involves belief *in* your nation, it does, indeed, share part of the psychology of religious belief. It is hard to believe in your nation, though, unless you appraise at least some of its achievements highly. Patriotism does not require you to believe that your nation is better, let alone best, among nations. But it works well, I think, only when you believe there is something distinctive in your national story to feel especially proud of, as Kang was proud of China's Confucian traditions.

THE GREAT UNBINDING

The speed of footbinding's demise remains astonishing. Gerry Mackie, after reviewing what statistics we have, concludes that, "footbinding started to end in China between the Boxer Rebellion of 1900 and the Revolution of 1911, certainly among the upper strata of the larger cities. Although there was local variability in onset of cessation, available evidence is that whenever binding did end, it ended rapidly." Footbinding trickled on well into the twentieth century here and there; but this millennial practice essentially disappeared in most places in a generation. "As measured by a sociologist's data," Mackie says, "the population of Tinghsien, a conservative rural area 125 miles south of Peking, went from 99 percent bound in 1889 to 94 percent bound in 1899 to zero bound in 1919."[65]

What, finally, brought it to an end? In a society in which pretty much all marriages were arranged, there was a very good reason not to give up footbinding your daughters until there were men ready to marry them. The genius of the strategy of the anti-footbinding societies was that it responded precisely to this difficulty; it created unbound unmarried women and men who would marry them at the same time. The double compact of the anti-footbinding societies—to refrain from binding your daugh-

ters' feet and from marrying your sons to foot-bound women—
did exactly what was required. And, in focusing on the contrast
between China and other places, it also made it clear that it was
possible to create societies—like Japan, but also like the Christian
missions—in which women were faithful, though unbound.

The mechanism that had made footbinding attractive to those
of lower social status depended on its being practiced by those of
higher social status. As a result, once enough men among the literati required unbound wives, there was inevitably a cascade down-
wards of unbinding that reversed the cascade of binding that had
spread the practice in the first place. Simply put, since footbinding
is embedded in a system of status, its abandonment by the elite
deprives it of its appeal; a mechanism that echoes in reverse the
case of the duel in England, where it was its uptake by people who
were not gentlemen that reduced its ability to secure gentlemanly
honor.

But to get this unraveling to start, you had to persuade enough
of the elite—enough of the Chinese literati and their families—
to abandon footbinding. Outsiders, along with Chinese educated
in Japan and the West, who opposed footbinding played a crucial role here. In drawing attention to the contrast between China
and the advancing industrializing world, at a time when some of
the literati had lost confidence in the capacity of their own traditions to defend them from modernizing strangers, they were able
to persuade some among the literati that they needed to promote
reform. Central to their story, as we can hear in their own words,
was the issue of the honor of their nation.

For many literati, this necessary reform came at a great price.
The anonymous writer of the "Secret Chronicle of the Lotus

Interest"—an essay that discusses frankly the erotic appeal of the bound foot—observed: "Our country's footbinding has become a type of backward practice in world history. Nowhere was woman confined more severely than through this. It should naturally be annihilated and become an unheard of phenomenon." But he went on, with a certain melancholy, "I did not mind using my energy to write this in order to indicate something of the utilities of the lotus and its holy mysteries, which survived a millennium."[66]

THREE

SUPPRESSING ATLANTIC SLAVERY

The unweary, unostentatious, and inglorious crusade of England against slavery may probably be regarded as among the three or four perfectly virtuous pages comprised in the history of nations.

—William Lecky, *History of European Morals*[1]

THE HONOR OF NATIONS

The Age of European Exploration, whose hinge moment was Columbus's "discovery" of the New World, had two great human consequences in the western hemisphere. One was the European settlement of the Americas, and the consequent destruction of Amerindian societies; the second was the transfer of Mediterranean traditions of plantation slavery to the islands and mainland of the vast landmass on the Atlantic's western rim. The development of the plantations required large supplies of labor in the tropics, labor that the aboriginal inhabitants of the region were not eager to provide. Accustomed as they were to its ecology and knowledgeable about its geography, it was relatively easy for them to escape from the control of the European settlers. Furthermore, great numbers of the Indians died from exposure to diseases that had developed in the Old World after their ancestors had come to the Americas, afflictions to which they had little natural immunity. If the plantation system was to develop, it needed an alternative source of labor.

Meanwhile, European engagement with Africa was growing, and because, at the time, many African societies were disrupted by internal warfare, captives were already in good supply. Over the centuries, once the demand for slaves in the New World was established, societies in West Africa developed economies based on slave raiding and trading, selling millions of people to the European slaving castles of the West African littoral. At the turn of the nineteenth century, the enslavement of non-European peoples was central to the Atlantic economy, connecting Europe, Africa, and the Americas. It was intricately bound up with the internal economies of many societies and was central to global trade. Few moral revolutions have been as consequential as the one that brought an end to the systematic enslavement of Africans and people of African descent in the Atlantic world.

The abolition of slavery was an extraordinary undertaking, its significance appreciated by thinkers around the world. Indeed, even in the debates over footbinding in China, progressive members of the literati would sometimes draw an analogy between their struggle and the movement to end Negro slavery in the West.

The parallels are not, I think, obvious. True, both abolitionism and the anti-footbinding movement were great, moralized campaigns against long-established traditions. But slavery was the subordination of one race by another and it entailed the systematic subjection of black people to dishonor; while footbinding, though its victims were all women, was practiced within the Han Chinese group and was a sign of elevated and not lowered status. Of course, the fact that footbinding was restricted to women reflected their subjection to men. Still, the inferiority of women did not mean they were dishonored. Indeed, women often carry the honor of their families—an issue to which we shall return in the next chapter—even though they do so in different ways from men.

There is another obvious contrast: slavery was very obviously not favored by slaves, whereas women generally supported and promulgated footbinding. But there is also one clear historical connection between slavery and footbinding. Their opponents, in

their respective cultures, saw both as threats to the honor of the
nations that authorized them.

The theme of national honor is inescapable in the literature
of abolition, as we shall see. But we shall also see that there were
other, more subterranean veins of argument in the debates about
the ending of Atlantic slavery, which connect honor with other
kinds of identity.

BRITISH HONOR AND THE SLAVE TRADE

The Parliament of the United Kingdom abolished the slave trade
in the British Empire in 1807; enacted the end of colonial slavery
in 1833; and abandoned the Negro Apprenticeship that succeeded
slavery in the West Indies in 1838, thus liberating, in the end,
more than three quarters of a million slaves. For a century after
these events, most British historians—indeed, most British people
who thought about it—saw this as the triumph of philanthropy
over self-interest. Then, in 1944, Eric Williams (who was later
to be the first prime minister of Trinidad and Tobago) argued, in
Capitalism and Slavery, that each step in the process of abolition
reflected the economic interests of Great Britain. It was a work in
the great Caribbean tradition of resistant Calibans. Williams's thesis was that the ending of the slave trade was a free trade measure
and the ending of slavery happened only when slave-produced
West Indian sugar was no longer profitable. As for the abolitionists, their humanitarianism was selective: they ignored the suffering of slaves outside the empire and of miners and agricultural
workers at home. The moral rhetoric of abolitionism was, in a
sense, a cover—what Winchilsea might have called a "blind"—for

the real economic interests in play.[2] Abolition, in sum, had nothing to do with philanthropy.

Williams's story fits with a view of politics as the rational pursuit of the self-interest of individuals or classes or nations; he endorsed a political "realism" that was skeptical about talk on what he called "the high moral or political plane."[3] And the great puzzle about abolition can be summarized in one simple observation: Williams was wrong. Far from being driven by British economic interests, abolition really *did* run against them; and this was clearly understood by those who championed it. We may be too cynical to agree with William Lecky's famous claim that "the unweary, unostentatious, and inglorious crusade of England against slavery may probably be regarded as among the three or four perfectly virtuous pages comprised in the history of nations." Yet it certainly was not the result of the operation of "self-interest, narrowly conceived."

Britain was a great maritime commercial empire, growing rich on its global trade, and the evidence that these decisions ran against its economic interests is now compelling. The supply of slaves from West Africa was at its peak in the era of abolition; prices were falling.[4] Though there were many who argued—in the spirit of Adam Smith—for the economic superiority of free labor, the experiments with freed slaves in Sierra Leone in the early nineteenth century hardly supported their claim. While Britain was engaged in the various stages of abolition, the products of slave labor were increasingly important in the global economy, and increasingly central to British consumption and production.

Seymour Drescher, one of the great historians of abolition, has argued persuasively not just that there was no economic reason to abandon slavery on the side of supply, but also that there was equally obviously no reason on the side of demand. The production of sugar—almost all of it by slaves—increased, with a brief fall as a result of the French and American revolutions, throughout the period from the 1780s (when, as we shall see, the first large-scale anti-slavery movement begins in Britain) until 1840, when abolition in the empire had basically been achieved.[5] Between 1787 and 1838, as he also points out, the proportion of cotton produced by slaves for the burgeoning English cotton industry rose from 70 percent to nearly 90 percent. In that period, there was no alternative supply of either commodity produced by free labor that could have taken up the slack.

William McNeill, a pioneer in global historical studies, once suggested that the growth in Britain's population at the turn of the nineteenth century made slave labor unnecessary, and that this accounted for the rise of anti-slavery sentiment. But the evidence does not support this view. If British overpopulation did the work, then we should expect that the net rate of migration out of England would have been lowest when slavery was established and highest when it was abolished. The reverse is true. As Drescher says: "British abolitionism 'took off' exactly when the net migration rate reached its tricentennial *low*."[6] In sum, Disraeli had a point when he offered his scornful summary of the anti-slavery campaigns in England: "The movement of the middle classes for the abolition of slavery was virtuous, but it was not wise."[7]

Lecky's famous praise of British virtue in his *History of European Morals*, with which I began this chapter, is preceded by a somewhat less familiar passage:

It is the merit of the Anglo-Saxon race that beyond all others it has produced men of the stamp of a Washington or a Hampden; men careless, indeed, for glory, but very careful of honor; who made the supreme majesty of moral rectitude the guiding principle of their lives, who proved in the most trying circumstances that no allurements of ambition, and no storms of passion, could cause them to deviate one hair's breadth from the course they believed to be their duty.[8]

There are many reasons we cannot accept his formulation, not least because it presupposes something we are by now in a good position to deny, namely, that being "careful of honor" is a sign of moral rectitude. As we saw with the history of the duel, honor and morality are separate systems: they can be aligned, as they may have been here; but, as we also saw, they can easily pull in opposite directions. Nevertheless, Lecky's insistence that honor matters in many ways to British abolition is, I shall try to persuade you, a central insight.

MORALITY IS NOT ENOUGH

To understand the abolitionist movement we need first to grasp that it required more than the conviction that slavery was morally wrong. What we have to explain here, as with footbinding, is why, in the political life of the nation, people came to act on that conviction. For anti-slavery sentiments were widely diffused well before the abolitionist movement really took off.

The spirit of the late eighteenth century ran against slavery for many reasons, starting with specifically Christian objections.

The Quakers, who believed that all men were equal in the eyes of God because all were equally capable of receiving His light, had opposed enslavement from early on. George Fox preached against holding slaves when he visited North America in 1671, and in 1775 the Society of Friends founded the world's first anti-slavery society in Philadelphia, whose honorary president from 1787 was Benjamin Franklin. More significant, at least in terms of numbers, was the Evangelical Revival within Anglicanism, which produced both the Methodism of the "lower orders," inspired by John and Charles Wesley's preaching from the 1740s, and the reforming spirit of the prosperous, educated Clapham Sect from the 1790s.

But slavery also offended the more secular spirits of the Enlightenment, whose opposition is epitomized in the article on the slave trade in Diderot and d'Alembert's *Encylopédie* (1751–77), the first modern encyclopedia. "If a trade of this sort can be justified by some principle of morals," it proclaimed, "there is no crime, however atrocious, that one could not legitimate."[9] Erasmus Darwin interrupted the argument of his *The Loves of the Plants* (1789)—an unlikely Enlightenment exercise in spreading scientific knowledge through poetry—with an apostrophe against slavery.

> E'en now in Afric's groves with hideous yell
> Fierce SLAVERY stalks, and slips the dogs of hell;
> . . . Hear him ye Senates! hear this truth sublime,
> "He, who allows oppression, shares the crime."[10]

Darwin himself was certainly not an Evangelical. (Indeed, in his *Zoonomia* he wrote, apropos of "the fear of hell": "Many theatric preachers among the Methodists successfully inspire this terror, and live comfortably upon the folly of their hearers.")[11] But the sentiment in Darwin's final line was one that echoed in Christian hearts. Whether they were Calvinists looking for evidence of their own predetermined divine election or Arminians concerned about losing God's grace, English Protestants in the late eighteenth century worried about the consequences of sharing *any* crime.[12]

By the mid-eighteenth century, then, both among the religious and the anti-religious, slavery was widely understood to be wrong. And so, as with the duel and with footbinding, what galvanizes the movement against slavery is not moral argument: the arguments are in place well before the movement begins.

It was the Quakers who began to organize these sentiments into a movement by petitioning Parliament for abolition in 1783. But here, too, there is something to explain. In the 1770s, the Quakers—though already insisting that abstinence from owning and trading slaves was a mark of their distinction—did not campaign publicly against slavery, even though, as we have seen, they had long repudiated it. This is hardly surprising. They were a small sect. In 1660, at the end of the Puritan Revolution, their numbers may have reached 60,000, but their membership declined significantly after that, and by 1800 the Society of Friends had perhaps 20,000 members.[13] Many of them were quite prosperous, and they depended for their security and their living on toleration in a society that (as we were reminded in the first chapter) made sworn allegiance to the doctrines of the Church of England a condition for public office. And yet in the 1780s Quakers took the lead in publicizing the evils of the slave trade.[14]

The Quakers' shift from abolitionism as a community ethos to abolitionism as a national campaign was a consequence of the movement's internal dynamics. They did so under pressure from American Quakers, led by Anthony Benezet of the Philadelphia Meeting; they had to do it, if they were to hold transnational Quakerism together, and solidarity—holding together—was one of their central values and concerns. They continued with abolitionism when they discovered, somewhat to their surprise, that their petition got a friendly reception, in part because no one had ever sent an anti-slavery petition to Parliament before and politicians could use the occasion to establish their humanity by praising the Quakers, while continuing to do nothing to prevent the trade. So far, honor was not at issue.

The London Quakers published *The Case of Our Fellow-Creatures, the Oppressed Africans* in 1784; and when it didn't produce a legislative response from Parliament, they orchestrated the first extensive anti-slavery campaign in Britain, seeding the British press with anti-slavery items.[15] What really worked, in the end, however, was the national campaign of petitions to Parliament, led by the Society for Effecting the Abolition of the Slave Trade, under the inspired leadership of Thomas Clarkson, Granville Sharp, and William Wilberforce (all of whom were Evangelical Anglicans).[16]

The Society organized petition-signing meetings all across the country, and they became competitive events. In the newly prosperous industrializing towns of the Midlands and the north—Birmingham, Stoke-on-Trent, Manchester—the campaign allowed new magnates, like Josiah Wedgwood, to express pride in their freshly acquired civic standing. Wedgwood, who was a close friend of Erasmus Darwin's (Susannah, his daughter, married Erasmus's son, Robert), made a great fortune by developing the first British industrial pottery factory at Burslem in Staffordshire. It was he who made and circulated the famous anti-slavery medallion of a kneeling African under the banner: "Am I not a man and a brother?" (And it was his great fortune that provided his grandson, Charles Darwin, the freedom to pursue his vocation as a naturalist.)

But if these were the leaders, the movement had huge numbers of followers among the "middling classes." (Late in 1787, in the first mass anti-slavery petition, the city of Manchester—with a population of just 50,000, counting children—produced almost 11,000 signatures.)[17] One measure of the movement's success was the fact that, in the early 1790s, between 300,000 and 400,000 people joined boycotts of slave-grown sugar—prompted by arguments such as those in William Fox's 1791 *Address to the People of Great Britain, on the Utility of Refraining from the Use of West India Sugar and Rum.*[18]

By the later eighteenth century, the novel in Britain was celebrating what Henry Mackenzie called, in the title of his novel of 1771, *The Man of Feeling*. The much-quoted apostrophe against slavery prompted by the episode with the caged starling in Laurence Sterne's *A Sentimental Journey* (1768) is typical of the new assumption that men, like women, should be moved—sometimes to tears—by suffering, including, in particular, the suffering of the slave.[19] "Looking up," Sterne writes,

> I saw . . . a starling hung in a little cage.—"I can't get out,—I can't get out," said the starling. . . . I fear, poor creature! said I, I cannot set thee at liberty.—"No," said the starling,—"I can't get out—I can't get out," said the starling.
>
> I vow I never had my affections more tenderly awakened; nor do I remember an incident in my life, where the dissipated

spirits, to which my reason had been a bubble, were so suddenly call'd home. . . .

Disguise thyself as thou wilt, still, Slavery! said I,—still thou art a bitter draught! and though thousands in all ages have been made to drink of thee, thou art no less bitter on that account.[20]

In adding your name to the tens of thousands of names on the petitions that rolled into Westminster, you could show yourself a man or woman of feeling, your "affections . . . tenderly awakened," a paragon of virtue. You could, in the final words of William Cowper's "Negro's Complaint" (written probably in 1788):

> *Prove that you have human feelings,*
> *Ere you proudly question ours!*[21]

LIBERTY: BRITAIN VERSUS AMERICA

But you could also see yourself upholding British honor. In the transatlantic polemics that led up to the Declaration of Independence, partisans of Britain made much of the claim that slavery was alien to British law. England was a country suffused with the rhetoric of the "free-born Englishman"; Lord Mansfield's decision in the Somerset case of 1772 (whatever it meant as a matter of technical law) was taken by friends and enemies of slavery alike to mean that a slave who stepped on British soil was at once a free man. The fact that the Americans were slaveholders, supporters of the British side could argue, made them unworthy of liberty. Those "who do not scruple to detain others in Slavery, have but a very partial and unjust claim to the protections of the laws of liberty," the anti-slavery campaigner Granville Sharp wrote in 1769 (and this was someone who actually supported American freedom from British rule).[22]

This argument hit home in the colonies for a simple reason: as the Reverend Morgan Godwin had pointed out years earlier, "*planters* have an extraordinary *Ambition* to be *thought well of.*" In 1786, Henry Laurens, the leading South Carolina slave importer, responded by comparing English protestations "to a pious, externally pious, Man's prohibiting fornication under his roof and keeping a dozen Mistresses abroad."[23]

The dynamic was straightforward, as the historian Christopher Leslie Brown points out in his magisterial study, *Moral Capital: Foundations of British Abolition*. British accusations of American hypocrisy about slavery were bound to produce American accusations of British hypocrisy about slavery. The Americans may have been slaveholders, but the British were slave traders. "In a similar way," Brown writes, "British denunciations of Caribbean slaveholding returned to Britain in the form of questions about daily injustices in England."[24] This is how the rhetoric of British antislavery as an organized political movement began.

The unexpressed premise of all these arguments was clear. As Brown puts it: "How individuals, communities, even nations conducted themselves with regard to human bondage could provide a legitimate standard for evaluating their politics. And only those who divested themselves from chattel slavery could rightfully campaign for political liberty."[25] Granville Sharp insisted on the point: slavery and the slave trade were, with other sins of empire, the source of "indelible disgrace." They were "a *National* undertaking, which may occasion the imputation of a *National* Guilt."[26] As one defends one's personal honor against other persons, one defends the national honor against other nations. Frederick Douglass, the great African-American abolitionist, got to the heart of the matter in a letter to Horace Greeley in 1845 explaining why he felt it important to campaign, as he was doing, in Britain, for American abolition. "Slavery exists in the United States because it is reputable, and it is reputable in the United States because it is not *dis*reputable out of the United States as it ought to be."[27]

British honor, colonial shame; the honor of Liverpool and Manchester; the honor of the newly empowered middling classes: these all helped mobilize the people who went beyond the moral commonplace that slavery was an evil and built a movement to compel Parliament to end the slave trade. Indeed, had the French Revolution and the associated rise of a Jacobin radicalism in Britain not intervened, Parliament might well have abolished the slave trade earlier than it did. But a government anxious about maintaining the authority of the ruling classes was cautious about large moves in a radical direction.[28] So it was not until 1807 that a British government, at war with a newly imperialist France under Napoleon, outlawed the British slave trade.

WILBERFORCE'S HONOR

National honor reemerged as a theme during the second phase of the British anti-slavery movement, when, after a pause of some fifteen years following the abolition of the slave trade, the organized assault on slavery itself begins. William Wilberforce opened his

1823 *Appeal to the Religion, Justice, and Humanity of the Inhabitants of the British Empire in Behalf of the Negro Slaves in the West Indies* with these words:

> To all the inhabitants of the British Empire, who value the favor
> of God, or are alive to the interests or honor of their country—
> to all who have any respect for justice, or any feelings of human-
> ity, I would solemnly address myself.[29]

Wilberforce's appeal to British honor might seem a mere rhetorical flourish. He slips it in after duty to God and national interest, though all three come before the moral considerations of justice and humanity. But for Wilberforce and his Evangelical friends (the group that was known, with evident irony, as the Clapham Saints), there was no place for honor independent of religion and morality. In their ideal, shame came only from breaches of Christian duty (which coincided with morality) and honor lay in adhering to it.

Granted that they would all have agreed that honor should be subordinated to morality, the Clapham Saints might seem to have abandoned the system of honor altogether. But Wilberforce had an answer to the question how morality and honor fitted together. In 1797, well launched into a public career devoted to the promotion of virtue and the suppression of vice, he argued that Scripture teaches Christians to be wary of "the desire of human estimation, and distinction, and honor." When, however, "worldly estimation and honor . . . are bestowed on us unsolicited for actions intrinsically good, we are to accept them as being intended by Providence to be . . . a present solace, and a reward to virtue."[30]

Is this the same honor that actuated standard English gentlemen? Well, other people's regard can only be a "present solace"
and "reward" if it gives us pleasure: and that pleasure in being
esteemed is an essential part of the subjective experience of honor.
Wilberforce's worry is that our concern for the regard of others
will inflame "our natural pride and selfishness." If we recognize
how unworthy we are in the sight of God, however, we will be
led to an "unfeigned humility." Even when what we do is rightly
admired, we should acknowledge that the glory is really due to
Him.[31] Quite how we combine obtaining solace from the esteem
of others with acknowledging that all honor is really due to God is
not, I think, satisfactorily explained.

St. Thomas Aquinas had provided, in one classical vision of
the matter, a wonderfully convenient shortcut: "honor is owed to
excellence. But the excellence of a man is judged above all according to his virtue. . . . And therefore honor properly speaking refers
to the same thing as virtue" (*Summa theologica*, 2a, 2ae, 145, 2).
In the world of the fallen, however, honor has an ungovernable
streak: it will not long submit to the dominion of virtue. That's
why so many religious writers worried about how they might
come to terms with it.

Where virtue and honor conflicted, Wilberforce, who was
appalled when his friend William Pitt took up his dueling pistols, knew which to follow. But from the same Christian perspective, collective honor could wield moral power, for the standard to
which the nation was being held in the name of honor was Christian rectitude. Even if a preoccupation with individual honor was
self-regarding, Wilberforce saw, an attention to national honor
could take us beyond our selves. Once you conceive of your honor

as the honor of an Englishman, it can lead you to patriotism, to heroism and self-sacrifice for a greater cause.

The Clapham Saints, then, could participate in the structures of honor, albeit in this highly moralized form. Esteem in the eighteenth century very often presupposed a social hierarchy of some sort, as we have seen; but we learn from Wilberforce that the standard that esteem presupposes can be a moral one. More than this, a morally engaged group can create an honor world of its own. Wilberforce and his Evangelical friends spoke of their more latitudinarian aristocratic superiors in terms that suggested how easy it was for the pious outside the ranks of the nobility to condescend to their putative superiors. This is no doubt part of what Eric Williams had in mind in his endorsement of the opinion of Wilberforce's critics: there is "a certain smugness about the man, his life, his religion."[32]

APPEALS TO THE HUMBLER CLASSES

There was, it's worth emphasizing, much more than national honor at stake in British anti-slavery. Christian duty, the brotherhood of all mankind under the fatherhood of the God of Abraham: these were also central themes. The movement's first real success in 1807, with the ending of the British slave trade, had been due, in some measure, to Wilberforce's regular insistence that Britain's support for slavery undermined its claim to be a Christian nation. The same appeal—amplified, perhaps, by the further spread of the Evangelical spirit—is found in the 1820s, when the campaign turned from the slave trade to colonial slavery itself.

The third of the 1826 *Letters on the Necessity of a Prompt Extinction of British Colonial Slavery; Chiefly Addressed to the More Influential Classes* maintained that it was a Christian duty to abstain from using slavery's products (repeating an argument that had led those hundreds of thousands to boycott sugar in the first round of opposition to the slave trade in the early 1790s): "To be exempt from the crime of encouraging and perpetuating slavery, and to make atonement for past negligence, we must not only abstain ourselves from all farther consumption of its produce, but determine, to the utmost of our power, to engage others in a similar resolution."[33] And the anonymous author went on to make arguments—of a sort familiar to those of us who recall the debates about South African sanctions—that the boycotting of West Indian sugar would indeed help put an end to slavery rather than simply impoverishing the planters and leading them to treat their slaves with even greater inhumanity.

But in the fifth of these letters "to the more influential classes," the author proposes what looks like a new strategy. The letter is entitled "On the importance of associations for the purpose of obtaining the cooperation of the humbler classes." It describes the results of canvassing the workers of a manufacturing town and the cottages of the rural poor: "The cause of emancipation, has been pleaded in the Senate by the wise, the eloquent, the noble. Now, it is pleaded in the workshop and the cottage, by women and children." And, the author writes, the prospects for a national campaign, based on the experience thus far, are extremely hopeful: "The result of personal visits, among the poor and laboring classes especially, has been, that more than nine out of ten families have cheerfully adopted the resolution, entirely to abstain from the consumption of West India sugar." In a later epistle, he insists—the sentence is capitalized—that "SLAVERY COULD NOT LAST A YEAR IF THE MIDDLE CLASSES ONCE EXPRESSED A DECIDED OPINION AGAINST IT." But in this one, he points to the fact that too many among the upper and middle classes are aware of the horrors of slavery and nevertheless do nothing. By contrast, he says, "information to the humbler classes, on the subject in question, is not lost labor, like too much of that bestowed on their superiors in knowledge and station."[34]

These are the arguments of a polemicist. This account of eager and sympathetic laborers can hardly be a complete picture. But there really does seem to have been a significant body of anti-slavery activism among the "humbler classes" of Englishmen and women in the period between the end of the slave trade and the abolition of colonial slavery a quarter century later, and the question is why.

A NEW WORKING CLASS

We can begin by recalling a few elements of the story that the great British historian E. P. Thompson told of *The Making of the English Working Class*. The disputes over the suffrage, which were the background to the Wellington-Winchilsea duel, took place in an atmosphere of intense competition among the aristocracy, the middle classes, and the poor. The beginnings of the trade union movement, inspired by the Jacobinism of the last decades of the eighteenth century, had produced, by way of reaction, the Combination Acts of 1799 and 1800. Their aim was to prohibit such unions and their effect was to drive much radical middle- and working-class organization underground. When the Combination Acts were repealed in 1824, the newly legitimate unions almost immediately organized strikes that alarmed the Tories under Lord Liverpool and their friends in business. Hence the second quarter of the nineteenth century begins with the passage in 1825 of a new Combination Act.

In the early 1790s, artisans and workingmen joined a sprinkling of other radicals to form what they called "Corresponding Societies" in the cities and towns of England. Modeled on the Committees of Correspondence of the American Revolution— which recorded and distributed the decisions of various groups to like-minded fellows—they were central in articulating the need for political transformation. Beginning with the London Corresponding Society in 1792, they made the reform of Parliament and the extension of the suffrage their first order of business; and they were among the first victims of the earlier Combination Acts. In the agitations that led to the Great Reform Act of 1832, their successors managed to gather huge crowds to campaign for change.

In 1830, the Birmingham Political Union drew some 15,000 people to its founding meeting; by 1832 and the week of rioting between May 9 and May 15 when England seemed to be on the brink of revolution, pro-reform organizations were able to draw crowds of a couple of hundred thousand. Meetings such as these added to the pressure that led to these first parliamentary reforms; Parliament got used to the novel idea that it might respond to— rather than direct—the nation's judgments. This was not a precedent that conservatives thought wise. As Disraeli was to write later of the whole process of abolition, "an enlightened aristocracy who placed themselves at the head of a movement which they did not originate, should have instructed, not sanctioned, the virtuous errors of a well-meaning but narrow-minded community"; and the well-meaning community he had in mind was, as he said, the "middle classes."[35]

But the Great Reform Act, which received the royal assent in June of 1832, was a significant disappointment to those who hoped to see the enfranchisement of the working classes; indeed, since the new property qualifications excluded anyone who did not own or lease land worth at least ten pounds, it was, from this point of view, no reform at all. The Great Reform defined working-class identity, in part, through reaction—as the status of those the reform did not reach. In the years that followed, dissatisfaction grew; and the workingmen of England and their supporters organized in groups such as the Universal Suffrage Club, which began "at a General Meeting of the Central Committee of the Metropolitan Radical Unions, held at the True Sun Office, on Friday, the 10th June, 1836, for the purpose of founding a Working-Man's Club."

The club's aims suggest that a substantial pride in a working-class identity was something still in the making; but it also showed that you could appeal to a workingman as such and to the common interests of working people:

The objects. To elevate the moral, intellectual, and political character of the Working Classes; to afford them more opportunities for friendly intercourse with each other; and for forming a more substantial compact between them and such men of learning, and political and moral integrity, as are desirous of making common cause with their less affluent brethren for placing happiness within the reach of all;—to soften, and eventually to subdue, the asperity of the aristocracy and middle classes towards the working portion of the people;—to prove to all their enemies the fitness of the working classes to manage their own affairs, . . . and finally, to establish perfect equality in the making and administration of the laws, as the only guarantee for securing to industry and real merit their just reward, and of ensuring peace and plenty, universal security and happiness.[36]

The Universal Suffrage Club did not last long, perhaps because its treasurer was the erratic Irish radical Feargus O'Connor, not a workingman but a Protestant landowner from County Cork, who had lost his seat in Parliament in 1835 for failing to meet the property qualifications for membership. Later that year, O'Connor joined the London Working Men's Association, whose leader, William Lovett, was one of the six workingmen who joined with six members of Parliament to issue the People's Charter in 1838. The six principles of their charter, the elements of what came to be called Chartism, were central in shaping the political struggles over national reform for the next decade. Finally, the Chartist movement, now headed by an increasingly unstable O'Connor (in 1852 he was committed to an asylum as the result of a fracas in the House of Commons), collapsed after its last huge public meeting of tens of thousands of supporters in Kennington in 1848. As the spirit of revolution spread across Europe that spring and summer, England remained calm.

Much of the older historiography has focused on the hostility between supporters of the working class and abolitionists: a conflict epitomized in the writings of William Cobbett, which I will discuss in a moment. But, among the members of these workingmen's associations, we can find active supporters of abolition.[37] By the time of the Chartist movement, Thompson argued, a working-class consciousness had come into being. "To step over the threshold, from 1832 to 1833," he writes toward the end of his great *Making of the English Working Class*, "is to step into a world in which the working-class presence can be felt in every county in England, and in most fields of life." And he continues:

> The new class consciousness of working people may be viewed from two aspects. On the one hand, there was a consciousness of identity of interests between working men of the most diverse occupations and levels of attainment, which was . . . expressed on an unprecedented scale in the general unionism of 1830–4. . . . On the other hand, there was a consciousness of the identity of that interest of the working class, or "productive classes," as against those of other classes. . . .[38]

Whether or not—and in what sense—they yet formed a single class, working people were often xenophobic and, like the British middle and upper classes, they could be frankly racist about black people. Many of them were nevertheless against slavery. They were against it, I think, for the simplest of reasons: nothing more firmly expressed the idea that labor was dishonorable than Negro plantation slavery in the New World. And labor was what defined *them*. Slavery associated the natal alienation and dishonor of the slaves with the work they did in the plantations and the slave manufactories of the New World.[39] Its unequivocal meaning was that manual labor was to be equated with suffering and dishonor. That was why it could be used to speak of the sufferings of those who were not literally enslaved.

William Cobbett's *Weekly Political Register* was, for the first three decades of the nineteenth century, required reading for radicals of all classes, and for the literate artisans whose story is at the heart of Thompson's *Making of the English Working Class;* it was required hearing for many of their less literate brethren who had it read out loud to them in the workingmen's societies. Cobbett had fled to America for two years in 1817 (fearing imprisonment for sedition) and had spent a briefer time there earlier in his youth; and he regularly compared the situation of the rural poor in England, often unfavorably, to the situation of Negro slaves in the Americas. At the Hampshire village of Burghclere on Sunday morning, November 6, 1825—I am picking one from scores of examples—where the rain had given him "time to look at the newspapers," a story about the problems of cotton merchants in New York led him to observe: "The slaves who cultivate and gather the cotton are well fed. They do not suffer. The sufferers are those who spin it and weave it and color it. . . ."[40] And *they* were in England.

Cobbett argued often that the abolitionist elites had noticed too little of the suffering of the white agricultural laborers at home while they waxed lyrical about the sufferings of the Negro abroad; and he often used racist language when speaking of black slaves. On the eve of the abolition of the slave trade, he "fulminated against the *Edinburgh Review* liberals for advocating abolition of the slave trade" in 1805, reminding them of "the imprisonments, the beatings, the whippings, the tortures, the hangings, the mock-legal murders, that are inflicted on the white slave in certain parts of Europe";[41] and in 1806, he promised: "so often as they agitate this question, with all its cant, for the relief of 500,000 blacks; so often will I remind them of the 1,200,000 paupers in England and Wales."[42] His response to the reopening of Wilberforce's campaign—which began with the pamphlet of 1823 I cited earlier—was to address the emancipator directly:

> Wilberforce,
>   I have you before me in a canting pamphlet. . . . At present
> I shall use it only thus . . . to ask you what propriety, what sense,
> what sincerity, there could be in your putting forth this thing, in
> the present state of this country?[43]

Now Cobbett's endless reiteration of the idea that it was the English poor who were the real slaves, the real sufferers, may have been intended to drive a wedge between the interests of the slaves and the interests of the English working classes; but its effect was just as much to draw attention to the oppression they shared. By the end of the journey, when he was elected to the reformed Parliament in 1832, Cobbett—who won his Oldham seat running against a West Indian plantation owner—campaigned as an abolitionist, too.

DEMOCRACY AND HONOR

Cobbett's career as a radical journalist fits with a point I made earlier, apropos of the duel, about the role of newspapers in shaping working-class responses to aristocratic behavior. In drawing attention to the contempt for ordinary people implied by their exclusion not just from the duel but from the other prerogatives of gentlemen as well, the press exposed gentlemanly codes of honor to a democratic challenge. It is striking that honor codes have tended to give, at best, a second-class role to women; that they have favored the powerful and scanted the virtues of ordinary men and women. In the more democratic age that was emerging as the English working class came into being, people were bound to ask whether honor could be made consistent with the great modern discovery: the fundamental equality, in the eyes of morality, of all human beings.

A number of philosophers have recently argued that it is always a good idea, in discussions of equality, to ask, first, "equality of what?" This view has a great deal of merit as a philosophical proposal, but I think it is the wrong place to start historically. When equality became, with liberty and fraternity, one of the three great slogans of the French Revolution, it was not because people had a clear idea what it was they wanted equality of. What they knew for sure was what they were *against*: treating people badly merely because they were not born into the nobility, looking down your nose at the common people. The ideal of equality in modern times begins, in short, with the thought that there are certain things that are *not* a proper basis for treating people unequally, and only gradually moves on to identify some things that *are*. Discrimination, in the sense of making distinctions in how we treat people on the basis of their social identities, began to need justification. So, for example, after the French and American revolutions, people started to challenge the notion that social status at birth was a proper basis for discrimination; and, over the last century, race and gender came to be increasingly recognized as illegitimate bases for discrimination as well.

As these ideas about what is not an adequate ground for discrimination developed, there emerged ideas about what is. One idea—the meritocratic idea—is that employment opportunities should be assigned not on the basis of status or connections but on the basis of talent. But employment is only one—though clearly a crucial one—of the contexts in which issues of equality arise. Equality also matters in other areas of our common life, in our governmental institutions, in courts and administrative bureaucracies, and in public discussion.

As to what equality positively requires, we might consider an idea that starts, again, in the democratic revolutions but reaches global significance with the Universal Declaration of Human Rights, in 1948. This idea is critical for how we should think about honor in our age. It's what we now call "dignity."

The Universal Declaration starts, in the first sentence of its preamble, by insisting that "recognition of the inherent dignity . . . of all members of the human family" is "the foundation of freedom, justice and peace in the world."[44] To most thinkers before the democratic revolutions, the idea of the inherent dignity of each person would have seemed absurd. An edition of Dr. Johnson's dictionary published about the time of Wellington's duel defines "dignity" as "elevation of rank; grandeur of mien; elevation of aspect. . . ."[45] None of these could be inherent in everyone, given that they are things that some people have because others do not. "Elevation of rank" is something that you can have only if others are ranked below you. As Edmund Burke argued in 1790, responding to the "oratorical flourish" of a revolutionary French politician who claimed that "all professions were honorable":

> In asserting that anything is honorable, we imply some distinc-
> tion in its favor. The occupation of a hair-dresser, or of a working
> tallow-chandler, cannot be a matter of honor to any person,—to
> say nothing of a number of other servile employments.[46]

You do not need to know that a tallow chandler makes candles out of animal fat to grasp the general idea. Burke's fundamental point was one that Thomas Hobbes had made more succinctly many years earlier: "men are continually in competition for Honor and Dignity."[47] For thinkers like Hobbes and Burke, dignity, like honor, was something intrinsically hierarchical.

So whatever dignity is today, in these more democratic times, it has to be something other than what it was in the past. That close connection between honor and dignity, which is evident in Hobbes's coupling of them, suggests a place to look in thinking about what has happened to dignity, namely to the connection between dignity and respect.

One way to understand what has happened to the word "dig-nity" is to say that it has come to refer to a right to respect that people have simply in virtue of their humanity. Here are a few of the facts about people that we give proper weight to in acknowl-edging human dignity: that human beings have the capacity for creating lives of significance; that we can suffer, love, create; that we need food, shelter, and recognition by others. And these facts, which we might dub the *grounds* of dignity, make it appropriate to respond to people in ways that respect such fundamental human needs and capacities.[48] Recall Stephen Darwall's distinction between recognition respect and appraisal respect. Much of the time, we've been discussing the forms of respect—what I have been calling "esteem"—that come from positive appraisal. Dignity, in its modern sense, has become a right to recognition respect, where we simply give appropriate weight to these crucial facts about people.

Some people think only hierarchical forms of the right to respect should be called "honor." There's a reason for this, beyond the insistence of a committed defender of social hierarchy like Edmund Burke: many of the most noticeable forms of honor from the *Iliad* to the Pashtunwali are, indeed, hierarchical. The issue here is not just a matter of a terminological stipulation, though: I think that much is to be gained by thinking about hierarchical and non-hierarchical codes that assign the right to respect together. The argument for that view is this book.

What is democratic about our current culture, then, is that we now presuppose all normal human beings, not just those who are especially elevated, to be entitled to respect. But granting everyone recognition respect is perfectly consistent with granting greater appraisal respect to some than to others, because these are different forms of respect. From now, I'll reserve the term *dignity* for one species of honor, namely, the right to recognition respect. So now we can say: Honoring some especially is consistent with recognizing the dignity of everyone else. Such dignity does not require the comparative forms of appraisal that go with more competitive forms of honor. It's not something you *earn*, and the appropriate response to your dignity is not pride so much as self-respect; after all, if your humanity entitles you to respect, then it entitles you to respect even from yourself!

There are important differences between dignity, understood this way, and other forms of honor; but the two have something important in common. If you fail to act in a way consistent with your dignity, people will rightly cease to respect you. You do not have to earn your human dignity—you do not have to do anything special to get it. But if you fail to live up to your humanity, you can lose it. In this respect, it is like Prince Hal's royal honor, which he did nothing to earn except show up, but which he could have lost by failing to live up to the standards it entailed. And if you lose your dignity, as with your honor, what you should feel is shame.

That comparative honor is conceptually distinct from dignity does not guarantee that it poses no threats to dignity. But if you worried about whether a culture of esteem might leave no place for respect for those who have done nothing special, the concept of "dignity" provides a modern answer. What follows from a commitment to human dignity, I think, is that we should take care to avoid creating honor worlds and honor codes that grant so much standing to the successful that they imply a disrespect for the rest of us.

In a society that denied respect to working people, claiming a dignity for them was a radical proposition. As the arguments for the equal dignity of the working classes developed, women, too, began to argue and then to organize for a place of greater respect in public life. In each of these movements—for the political equality of workingmen and then of all women—the goal was not comparative honor, which depended on special achievement, but dignity, based in grounds that women and working-class men could rightly argue they shared with gentlemen. And to get it, both workers and women took part in highly visible, organized, public campaigns.

THE DIGNITY OF LABOR

In recalling the energy of the abolitionists it is important to remember the extraordinary scale of their mobilization. Abolitionism was by far the most active subject of petition to the government in the half a century between the opening salvo against the slave trade and the Abolition Bill. In 1829, Seymour Drescher notes, English petitioners ran five to one against Catholic emancipation; in 1833, signatures ran seventy-five to one in *favor* of immediate abolition.[49] Perhaps the most impressive way of thinking about the numbers is to point out, as Drescher does, that it is likely that more than 20 percent of British men over the age of fifteen signed the anti-slavery petitions of 1833. To sign up that proportion of the male population of that age in the United States in 2010, you would have to persuade more than 23 million people, and you would have to do it without the resources of the Internet!

Part of the excitement of the anti-slavery campaign was the continuous round of lectures and meetings, in towns and villages, that the abolitionists organized. The British historian James Walvin has described countless meetings around the British Isles, filled to overflowing, as the campaign for the Abolition Bill reached its climax.

•

In May 1830 the General Meeting of the Anti-Slavery Society attracted a meeting of 2000 with 1500 unable to enter. Much the same story was repeated wherever anti-slavery societies met—as far afield as Cork. In Leeds it was claimed that 6000 people filled the local Colored Cloth Hall. When in the New Year 1831 a similar meeting was called in Edinburgh, *The Scotsman* thought it "one of the largest and most respectable meetings ever assembled in that intellectual city."

In small towns, too, with resonant English names—Woburn, Newport Pagnell, Baldock, Hitchin—the halls were filled to overflowing.[50] In its 1831 report, the Agency Committee, which managed the campaign, recorded that it had appointed five lecturers "to prepare the way for a general expression of public feeling, when the time shall arrive, by widely disseminating an accurate knowledge of the nature and effect of Colonial Slavery."[51] The knowledge they disseminated was to be not just accurate but extensive: meetings might last six or seven hours, and, though the local dignitaries had their say, the Agency speaker might consume as many as three of them.

It was these campaigns that roused Britons to produce 1.5 million signatures in the final parliamentary session before abolition in 1833. You could not produce these numbers without appealing to all classes. English men and women, whatever their class, had some argument of honor to bring them to the petition table ready to sign. They were prepared to testify before their neighbors and before their parliamentary leaders that freeborn Englishmen were united in their abhorrence of slavery, and in so doing, they could claim their share of the nation's honor. In taking part in these great public rituals of the 1830s, working people could claim their right to respect *as* working people, in the way that the industrialists of the Midlands and the north had sought respectability for their towns (and their class) in the anti-slave-trade movement of an earlier generation. The new working class had economic interests, certainly, and we can debate whether or not those interests were aligned with the slaves': but working-class people needed, as we all do, to live with an image of themselves that allowed them self-respect.

Honor figures, then, in at least three ways in British abolition. First, national honor played a central role in the debates about abolition. Second, the honor of the newly industrializing cities of the Midlands and the north of England led its citizens—both high and middling—to compete in the race to send the earliest or the largest petitions to Parliament. These claims, I think, would be endorsed by most who have explored these issues. But I want to add to these more widely accepted explanations, the thought that the participation of British workers was connected with a new symbolic investment in their own dignity.

As Hegel understood, though human consciousness can be self-directed, it also involves a dialogue with the consciousnesses of others. Sometimes in talk of honor, it is the self-respect of those seeking honor as much as the respect of others that matters. The concern for the dignity of labor among the laboring classes had as much to do with how they thought of themselves as with how they were regarded by others. For many of them, slavery rankled. Not simply because, as Britons, they cared about the nation's honor, not just as a matter of Christian conscience, and not because they were in competition with the slaves (they were not). It rankled because they, like the slaves, labored and produced by the sweat of their brow.

Two decades after British abolition, the settled consensus in the

United Kingdom about the wrongness of slavery had huge practical consequences. In Great Britain at the onset of the American Civil War, there was enormous sympathy among the conservative aristocracy for the Southern plantation owners with whom they identified. As London's *Morning Star* put it on May 12, 1862, "an aristocracy of blood acknowledge[d] kinship with an aristocracy of color."[52] Nevertheless, the British did not intervene on the side of the Confederacy. Had they done so, as Lord Palmerston's cabinet actually considered doing, the outcome of the Civil War might well have been very different. Once the Emancipation Proclamation of 1863 allowed the supporters of the North to conceive the war simply as a struggle against slavery, though, both working-class and middle-class opinion stood in the way of upper-class thoughts of intervention.[53] The landed aristocracy was no longer the ruling class. As the British Empire expanded through the nineteenth century, the abolition of forms of slavery indigenous to Africa and to Asia came to be one of the aims of imperial policy.

On August 17, 1846, at the Crown and Anchor in London's Strand, Frederick Douglass and William Lloyd Garrison (the leading black and white American abolitionists of their day) joined William Lovett and Henry Vincent—founder and leading orator, respectively, of the Chartist London Working Men's Association— to announce a new Anti-Slavery League. The League was an attempt to create a British base for the more radical Garrisonian wing of American abolitionism, and it fizzled out less than a year later.[54] But on that August night, as Garrison and Douglass gave the fiery speeches they were known for to a rapturously appreciative audience, there was a brief moment when you could have imagined an international alliance between British working people and the 3 million American slaves, struggling together for the dignity of labor. In a room where Boswell and Johnson had quaffed their liquor, the earnest assembly of teetotalers listened as Vincent—whom Sir Henry Molesworth had called "the Demosthenes of the new movement"—brought the six-hour-long meeting to a close with a speech about the shared cause of the slaves and the British working class. One of Douglass's biographers writes wistfully of the failure of the Anti-Slavery League to create an international movement of working people as "one of the great missed opportunities of Douglass's life."[55]

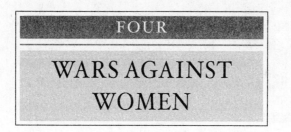

FOUR

WARS AGAINST WOMEN

What sort of honor is it to open fire on an unarmed woman?

—Asma Jahangir[1]

SEDUCED AND ABANDONED

In Pietro Germi's film comedy *Sedotta e Abbandonata* (1964), which is set in a small town in Sicily, fifteen-year-old Agnese Ascalone is "seduced and abandoned" by her sister's fiancé, Peppino Califano.[2] When her father, Don Vincenzo, finds out, he rushes over to the Califano family home, hoping to persuade them that the families must make a small alteration in their plans; rather than marrying the older sister, Peppino should marry the younger one. Eventually, the young man's father, Signor Califano, gives his word. He understands that Don Vincenzo has his family honor to defend. But Peppino is unwilling, and runs off (with his parents' blessing) to hide out with one of his cousins.

In the ensuing brouhaha, Agnese's brother is sent to find and shoot Peppino, fails, and is caught. The judge charges him with attempted murder, and Peppino with corrupting a minor; the only way the two young men can avoid prison is for Peppino and Agnese to get married. Local custom offers a simple solution: Peppino and a few of his friends must stage a very public kidnapping of Agnese. That way, his private seduction, which cannot be publicly acknowledged, can be replaced with this public pretext for the wedding. Everyone assumes that the community will agree, after the kidnapping, that the two young people have to get married to preserve the honor of Agnese and her family.

From time to time, in the course of the film, we see Police Chief Polenza, a mainland Italian, expressing his exasperation at the to-ing and fro-ing of the Ascalones and the Califanos and bemoaning the crazy world of Sicilian honor. (In one scene at the police station, he looks at a map of Italy and covers the island of Sicily with his hands, muttering, "Better, much better," imagining how much his homeland would be improved by the disappearance of this annoying excrescence.) When he gets wind of the kidnapping plan, Polenza knows what to do. He decamps with the young policeman who shares his responsibilities for maintaining the law, leaving town so they can avoid the whole messy business.

On a blistering afternoon, they lie in the shade of an olive tree in the hot Sicilian sun, and the older man tries to explain what is going on to his young assistant, Bisigato (who is played by an actor whose striking blondness underlines the fact that he, too, is not Sicilian).

POLENZA: He's kidnapping the girl today. What would you do?

BISIGATO: Arrest him immediately.

POLENZA: Great. So he can marry her tomorrow and go scot-free, while you look like a fool. Get it through your head. Marriage nullifies it all: kidnapping, rape, corruption of a minor. It's all in Article 544. Marriage wipes the slate clean. Better than an amnesty. You didn't know? Kids around here learn it with their catechism.

BISIGATO: Why not just marry her?

POLENZA: He doesn't want her.

BISIGATO: Then why kidnap her?

POLENZA: So he's forced to marry her. They're all in on it.

BISIGATO: But not him?

POLENZA: Yes, he's in on it too.

BISIGATO: With all due respect, sir, I don't understand.

POLENZA: You can't, Bisigato. It's a question of honor. It's always a
question of honor.

Sedotta e Abbandonata is a funny film about a very serious business.
Don Vincenzo's obsession with the good name of the Ascalones
presupposes one of the commonest ideas about honor across the
globe: in many, many, societies, if a young woman has sex before
she is married, not only her honor but that of all her family is
besmirched.

This is not just a matter of their sentiments, of the pride and
shame of the Ascalones. If Don Vincenzo doesn't solve the problem in a way that recovers his family honor, his other daughters
and his son will not be able to have respectable marriages, he himself will be mocked, his wife will be pitied. He will not be able
to stand tall in his community. He will have lost the respect of
all his peers. In his world, there is only one way out: the seducer
must marry his younger daughter (and Don Vincenzo must look
for another husband for her elder sister). When Peppino tries to
escape this fate, the same code then requires one of the Ascalone
men to kill him.

The level of paternal violence in the Ascalone family will star-
tle some contemporary viewers. Don Vincenzo beats his daughters
and his son; he bullies his wife. Mostly, she does not try to stop
him beating their children. Mostly, they seem to take it for granted
that their father's authority must be maintained with his angry
tirades and his brutal fists. Masculinity in this world is defined by
the capacity for violence. Even Agnese's mildly effeminate brother
is required to go after Peppino, however reluctantly, with a rifle.

To insist on the obvious: the code that Don Vincenzo lives by makes very different demands of men and of women. The double standards of this system are nicely exposed in a scene around the Califano dinner table, where Peppino begs his parents not to make him marry the young woman who is carrying his child.

PEPPINO: Answer me this. In all honesty, would you have married Mama if she'd done what Agnese did with me?

FATHER: What's that got to do with it?

MOTHER: You tried to get me to.

FATHER: So? It's a man's right to ask and a woman's duty to refuse.

PEPPINO: Exactly. Agnese didn't refuse, did she? . . . I won't marry that whore.

FATHER: I gave Don Vincenzo my word!

MOTHER: You didn't answer his question. If I'd given in, would you have married me?

FATHER: Certainly not!

The code assumes any man is always free to seek sex with women to whom he is not married and that it is the woman's "duty to refuse." That is why, if the man succeeds, the dishonor attaches to the woman: only she has broken the rules. Peppino desires the beautiful Agnese. He desperately wants to have sex with her. But if she agrees to sex outside marriage, she is a "whore"; and so he cannot marry her, even if she has had sex only with him, even if she is carrying his child.

In those days, Article 544 of the Italian criminal code, which the chief of police mentions, recognized a kind of marriage—the *matrimonio riparatore*—that "repaired" the wrong done by rape, even of a minor. (This is an old idea, which you can find in Deuteronomy [22:28–29]:

> If a man find a damsel that is a virgin, which is not betrothed, and
> lay hold on her, and lie with her, and they be found; Then . . .
> she shall be his wife; because he hath humbled her, he may not
> put her away all his days.)

And the *matrimonio riparatore* was not just a plot device in the movies. The day after Christmas of 1965 (a little more than a year after *Sedotta e Abbandonata* first appeared), a young woman named Franca Viola, who was just seventeen years old, was kidnapped and raped by Filippo Melodia, a petty crook, in the small Sicilian town of Alcamo. Her attacker was assisted by a dozen of his male friends. She had repeatedly rejected his advances in the past. But, as Signor Polenza anticipated, Melodia had learned "with his catechism" that, once they had sex, she would recognize that the only way to save her family honor was for her to marry him. And, once they married, Article 544 would protect him from any legal consequences of the rape.

Filippo Melodia turned out to have underestimated Franca Viola. She told her family she would not marry him and, with the support of her father, she insisted on pressing rape charges. Her family endured ostracism and exactly the sort of loss of respect that is the price of diverging from the codes of honor. Because they contested the code, her father also faced death threats and the family's barn and vineyards were set aflame. Nevertheless, the prosecution went ahead and Melodia and seven of his confederates were imprisoned. Three years later, Ms. Viola married Giuseppe

Ruisi, her childhood sweetheart, the man she had been engaged to since the age of fourteen: at the wedding, he had to carry a gun to protect them.[3]

The larger reverberations of the event cannot be doubted. The national media covered their ceremony. The president of Italy sent them a wedding present. Pope Paul VI gave them an audience.[4] The young couple moved away from Alcamo for the first few years of their marriage, but in the early 1970s Franca Viola and her husband Giuseppe returned there. She has largely stayed away from the limelight in the ensuing years, living a normal life in Alcamo; but in 2006 she told an interviewer that her advice, when faced with an important decision, was "to follow always your own heart."[5]

Franca Viola was raped at the age of seventeen; she was almost twice that age when Article 544 was finally repealed in 1981.

MURDEROUS FAMILIES

Elsewhere in the world (as in earlier times), the penalty for the dishonor that comes with the loss of female virginity before marriage is often much more severe. In the film, Agnese accepts the fate that Franca Viola escaped: she is forced into a marriage with a man who has treated her with contempt. But in many places and periods, restoring the family honor would have required killing not only the man who seduced her but the girl herself as well. Indeed, in Sicily, as in may other societies, both Christian and Muslim, in the Mediterranean world, that was—and in some of those places still is—what the code requires. In certain communities, a young woman loses her honor and earns this murderous penalty, even if, like Franca Viola, she was raped.

Now, the code that governs these so-called honor killings has elements that are surely recognizable to most people around the world. Even in the industrialized West, in the United States and in Europe, it has taken an enormous amount of work to persuade women and men that rape should not be treated as a source of shame for the victim. It's not that women who have been raped believe deep down that they were "asking for it"; the shame has, instead, to do with the powerlessness of being a victim. It is not guilt—the thought that they have done something wrong—that haunts them, it is the reminder of their humiliation. And that humiliation—the fact that, as Deuteronomy puts it, the rapist has humbled his victim—makes it possible that she will lose the respect of those who know she was raped, however unreasonable this may be; indeed, it may undermine (once more, for no good reason) her respect for herself.

The assumption that because you cannot resist the physical imposition of another you have been shown to be inferior in some more general way is very widespread (and not just in connection with sexual assault). Within this system of attitudes and feelings is the trace of the idea that women who have been raped, like men who have been bested in an assault, have lost their honor. Weakness—even in the face of iniquity—is a source of shame.

In the United States, it is also true to this day that many parents and families worry more about the sexual adventures of unmarried daughters than of sons. This is rationalized by pointing out that the girl has more at stake—pregnancy changes the life of a girl in ways it doesn't change the life of the boy. I suspect that what many people really think, though, is what Peppino and his father thought: "It's a man's right to ask and a woman's duty to refuse." Self-restraint is unmanly; resistance is appropriately feminine.

But whatever our thoughts and feelings about sex outside marriage, most of us cannot make sense of someone who thinks the right response to an unmarried daughter who chooses to have sex, or a married daughter who commits adultery, is to kill her; least of all can we understand someone who kills a daughter or sister, married or not, who has been raped.

And yet, according to an estimate in a UN report in 2000, as many as 5,000 women and girls are murdered each year by relatives for just such reasons.[6] These murders are called "honor killings" because they are seen by their perpetrators as ways of reestablishing the family's honor, which has been lost by extramarital sexual activity, willing or unwilling, on the part of one of its female members. In Pakistan in 2003, according to an adviser to the country's prime minister, as many as 1,261 women were murdered in this way. (There is widespread agreement that these official figures understate the extent of the devastation.)[7]

So far we have been exploring revolutions that are over. In this chapter I turn to the present and to an honor practice where change is desperately needed. The search for an understanding of honor killing requires, like the understanding of any honor world, an attempt to make sense of its codes. And while there is a general pattern to honor killings across cultures, it is in the specifics of particular place and time that we will be able to see best what is at stake. But we can also learn something, as we'll see, from the histories we have already explored. So I aim here to put our new understanding of honor in the service of a proposal as to one way we might make progress against honor killers. Pace that cynical French maxim, *tout comprendre* is not always *tout pardonner*.

THE LIFE AND DEATH OF SAMIA SARWAR

In 1989, Ghulam Sarwar Khan Mohmand, one of the most successful businessmen in Peshawar, capital of Pakistan's North-West Frontier Province (NWFP), threw a grand wedding for his daughter Samia. Over a thousand guests gathered for the celebration, among them three of Pakistan's provincial chief ministers, one federally appointed governor, and much of the city's business elite. The bridegroom, Imran Saleh, was the son of his wife's sister. This was a modern, successful Pashtun family: Ghulam Sarwar Mohmand's wife, Sultana, was a doctor, as was her nephew Imran. Samia Sarwar studied law later; her sister went on to study medicine. In 1998, Sarwar himself was to be elected to the first of two terms as president of Peshawar's Sarhad Chamber of Commerce and Industry.[8]

Despite these auspicious beginnings, the marriage was not a success. Samia Sarwar told her lawyer later that her husband was extremely abusive, and her parents eventually accepted that she should leave him, allowing her to move back in with them in 1995, when she was pregnant with her second son. Dr. Saleh called sometime later to say that he did not want her to come back. She never saw him again. But her parents were adamant that a divorce was out of the question. "You can get anything you want here," she said they told her, "except a divorce."[9] The reason was straightforward: a divorce would threaten their *ghairat*, the family's honor.[10] As in Sicily, the practical consequences of a loss of honor here in northern Pakistan would include difficulty in arranging a marriage for her sister and her cousins, and social difficulties for her parents and her aunts and uncles.

Sometime in the years that followed—with her husband long out of the picture—Samia Sarwar apparently fell in love with another man. She was now a law student and so she certainly knew that she had the legal right to petition for divorce from a husband who had first abused and then abandoned her. In March 1999, while her parents were away in Mecca, making the Hajj, she fled to Lahore. She moved into Lahore's only private refuge for battered women, Dastak, and made arrangements with the Pakistani human rights lawyer Hina Jilani to begin divorce proceedings against her husband.

Over the next few weeks, the Sarwars persuaded their daughter and her lawyer that they were finally willing to agree to the divorce, showing the necessary papers to a prominent opposition politician, who passed on the good news. And so, on April 6, 1999, she agreed to meet with her mother—she was not willing, she said, to deal with her father—at her lawyer's office. Her mother was supposed to come alone, but when she arrived she was on the arm of a stocky, bearded man. According to Hina Jilani, Mrs. Sarwar said this was her driver, whose help she needed because she couldn't walk on her own.[11]

Once the two of them entered the office over the lawyer's objection, the driver, Habibur Rehman, pulled out a gun and shot Samia Sarwar in the head. In the ensuing panic, Rehman was himself shot dead by a security guard, and Samia's uncle, Yunus Sarwar, who had been waiting outside, kidnapped one of the paralegals in the office, and drove off with her and Samia's mother in a taxi. The paralegal said later that Mrs. Sarwar was "cool and collected during the getaway, walking away from the murder of her daughter as though the woman slumped in her own blood was a stranger."[12] In Pakistan, alas, you would do best not to listen to Franca Viola's advice about "following your heart."

The protagonists in this drama were all prominent Pakistanis. Hina Jilani, one of Pakistan's leading human rights lawyers, shares her legal practice with her sister, Asma Jahangir, head of Pakistan's Human Rights Commission and Special Rapporteur of the UN Commission on Human Rights on Extrajudicial, Summary or Arbitrary Executions. (Ms. Jahangir apparently had to delay her departure for a meeting in Geneva to help deal with the consequences of this extrajudicial killing in her own office.) The intermediary whose review of the supposed divorce papers had led Ms. Sarwar to agree to the meeting was Aitzaz Ahsan, a distinguished lawyer and former minister of justice, who was at the time the Leader of the Opposition in the Senate.

Since Samia Sarwar was exercising her legal right to seek a divorce when she was murdered in front of witnesses, and since murder is, of course, illegal in Pakistan, you might have expected universal condemnation. Benazir Bhutto and a number of Pakistan's other progressive political leaders did speak out against it; and there were public protests by human rights organizations the next day in several of Pakistan's major cities.[13] But when a member of Pakistan's Senate moved a resolution to condemn the family, the response was not what he must have hoped for.

The senator in question—Iqbal Haider, the lawyer and human rights activist, of the progressive Pakistan People's Party—was condemned by his parliamentary colleagues from the NWFP, especially by members of the Awami National Party (ANP), which draws its strength from the Pashtun areas of Pakistan, whose capital is Peshawar, home of the Sarwars. A defense of Pashtun traditions of honor might have been expected from that direction, except that the ANP was far from traditionalist: it was toward the secular end of Pakistan's political spectrum and it had been consistent in its opposition to the Taliban in the North-West Frontier Province. Senator Ajmal Khattak, who was at that time the party's president, is a leading Pashto intellectual and poet. He once had a reputation as a progressive figure, having supported leftist revolutionaries like Castro and Che Guevara.[14] Nevertheless, Khattak lectured his colleagues on Pashtun ideas of honor and appeared to defend honor killings.[15] Of only four senators who supported the motion, one was Aitzaz Ahsan, the senator who had been drawn into the affair when he agreed to mediate between Samia Sarwar and her family.[16]

In Peshawar, there was indignation at the fact that outsiders had interfered in the affairs of a local family: Pashtun honor had been impugned by meddling strangers. The chamber of commerce of which Samia's father was the president issued an attack on Hina Jilani and Asma Jahangir, urging that they be punished under "tribal and Islamic law" for "misleading women in Pakistan and contributing to the country's bad image abroad." Several religious leaders in the NWFP issued fatwas declaring the two women to be infidels.[17] No one has ever been convicted in connection with Samia Sarwar's murder and her father remains a prominent figure in Peshawar. In November 2009, Pakistan's Ministry of Commerce appointed him to a committee to advise them on a new trade agreement with Afghanistan.[18]

THE WAY OF THE PASHTUNS

More than 40 million Pashtuns live in Pakistan and Afghanistan, most of them in the regions on either side of the border. Pashtuns think of themselves as the descendants of a single common ancestor, and their tribal organization is what anthropologists call a "segmentary lineage system," in which people act in solidarity with closer relatives against more distant cousins, according to the formula in the Bedouin proverb: "Me against my brothers, me and my brothers against my cousins, me and my brothers and my cousins against the world." The further back the common ancestor, the larger the group, of course, and the Pashtun kinship system has many levels of various scales that are important for practical life.

The four main tribal groupings derive, tradition asserts, from the immediate descendants of Qais Abdur Rashid, the man all Pashtuns claim as their forefather. Qais was apparently a contemporary of Muhammad's, who traveled to Mecca and brought Islam back to Afghanistan. The many immediate subdivisions of these four groups usually have a notional genealogy that goes back to one of Qais's descendants in the first few generations. At the bottom of this hierarchy is the smallest family group consisting of a man and his sons, their wives and their children and grandchildren.

In the countryside, the Pashtuns have traditionally lived by farming in small villages of a few score people, often belonging to a few such extended families. In the country and in the city, they live by a code of life they call the "Pashtunwali," or the way of the Pashtuns. Like many such tribal codes, it lays great stress on maintaining one's honor by loyalty to one's kin, bravery in battle, hospitality to guests, retaliation for insults, and revenge for injury, whether against oneself or against members of one's family or tribe.[19] One's own good name and that of one's family or tribe, captured in a rich vocabulary of terms for honor, some borrowed from Arabic, are at the heart of the Pashtunwali.

These ideas, which developed in a rural tribal culture, have been taken into contemporary urban life. After three decades of warfare in Afghanistan—beginning with the Soviet invasion at the end of 1979 and continuing with the American-led war against the Taliban—many Pashtuns in Pakistan identify strongly with their kinsmen across the border. And the presence of foreigners—both soldiers and civilians—apparently intent on reshaping the life of the region has produced an entirely predictable nationalist response. There is a great deal of insistence on the threat to the Pashtunwali posed by foreign pressure. In Pakistan, this pressure is seen, as well, in the activities of human rights groups that campaign for women's rights and oppose practices like honor killing. The result is a situation where criticism of the killing of Samia Sarwar even by homegrown Pakistani human rights activists, like her lawyer, Hina Jilani, produces a torrent of complaints about Western interference, at the heart of which is an insistence that Westerners are *bay ghairat*, lacking in a sense of honor.[20]

Samia Sarwar was Pashtun; but her murder could have occurred in any region of Pakistan. Among Urdu and Sindhi and Punjabi speakers, as with those who speak the smaller languages of the country, there are similar traditions. In the language of Sindh, the province that contains Karachi, Pakistan's financial capital and largest city, the word *karo* literally means "black man," and its feminine, *kari*, "black woman"; and these words are used to refer to people who have sex outside marriage. So *karo-kari* is one of the commonest names by which honor killings—which occur all over the country, as I say—are known in Pakistan; though the equivalent term in Pashto is *tor-tora*.[21]

We face here what is by now a familiar paradox. Pakistan is an Islamic republic, created to be a homeland for the Muslims of India after the communal conflicts prior to Indian independence. And there is almost universal agreement among qualified interpreters of Islam that honor killing is un-Islamic. Like dueling at its apogee, which ran contrary to law and religion in Christian Great Britain, honor killing is not only illegal in Pakistan, it is contrary to the official religious traditions of a country which, like Britain, has an established faith. One reason is that Islamic law has its own ways of regulating sexual modesty, and families who enforce their codes without going through the sharia courts, like the gentlemen who engaged in duels, are declaring their independence from the state's rules and from organized religion. Of course, Islam, like other world religions, has adopted particular inflections in the varied societies into which it has traveled. In the minds of its adherents, the Pashtunwali is completely compatible with Islam; indeed, they are inclined to think of Islam itself as one of the ways of the Pashtun, since they believe their founding ancestor brought the faith back from Mecca. But, as I say, it is widely agreed across the world of Islam that neither the Koran nor the Sunnah (the Prophet's usages) nor the hadith (the authoritative accounts of Sunnah that provide an additional source for teaching) endorse the killing of women by men in their own family.

There can be no doubt that this is well understood in Pakistan, in particular. In the summers of 2001 and 2002, Amir H. Jafri, a Pakistani graduate student working on a dissertation in communications, conducted a series of interviews in English and Urdu aimed at placing the killing of Samia Sarwar and the response to it in its fullest cultural context. He reports a fascinating conversation with a mullah named Abad at a mosque in Islamabad. To begin with, this religious teacher surrounded by his students admits that when he sees women who are not totally veiled, "I just want to cut them into bits or betroth them to someone . . ." When the startled Jafri asks if this is consistent with Islam, the mullah blushes and falls silent for a moment. Then, he looks around at his students and mumbles, "Islam does not allow it but sometimes you have to do it to set an example."

This interview was the only occasion over two summers of research in Pakistan in which Dr. Jafri was able to find a scholar of any of the sects of Islam who "overtly condoned" anything like honor killing.[22] The reality was nicely summarized once by a Pashtun taxi driver, in a discussion of women's education with an educated woman passenger: "I said, babaji, in Islam women and men are supposed to gain education, it's required for them. He said, yes, but who cares about Islam when it comes to *ghairat*?"[23]

Samia Sarwar's murder was not officially sanctioned by any authority outside her family. But in the North-West Frontier Province, honor killings are quite likely to be the results of decisions made by the *jirgas*, traditional courts that have extensive practical authority in the tribal areas, where the government of Pakistan's writ barely runs. A couple of weeks before Samia Sarwar was murdered, a sixteen-year-old mentally disabled young woman, whose name was Lal Jamilla Mandokhel, was executed after a "trial" by a *jirga* in her village. She had been raped repeatedly over two nights by a man in a nearby town. When she came back to her village, the elders of her community decided she had brought dishonor on her people. She was dragged from her home and shot, as a large crowd looked on.[24] Whether or not it is consistent with Islam, honor killing is, in many places, part of the way of the Pashtuns.

THE LAWS OF PAKISTAN

Pakistan's modern legal system began as a colonial inheritance. Muhammad Ali Jinnah, the founder of Pakistan, was a British-trained lawyer and he was probably himself in favor of a secular constitution. But Jinnah died soon after the British recognized the Partition of India in 1947, granting India and Pakistan their separate independences. Pakistan consisted, at first, of two geographically isolated parts, one in the west and a culturally rather different region in Bengal, far to the east. It took nearly a decade for the Constituent Assembly that was effectively the parliament of Pakistan during this period to agree on a constitution, and when it did, in 1956, it was the constitution of an Islamic republic. In the decades that followed, through a series of coups and a war in which the two halves of Pakistan became the two independent states of Pakistan (in the west) and Bangladesh (in the east), the fundamental law of Pakistan was always officially Islamic. The current constitution, ratified in 1973, borrows its preamble from earlier constitutions, which state that the fundamental law aims to "establish an order" wherein

the Muslims shall be enabled to order their lives in the individual and collective spheres in accordance with the teachings
and requirements of Islam as set out in the Holy Quran and
Sunnah. . . .[25]

The constitution also creates a federal Shariat Court, composed
both of traditional Muslim legal scholars, or *ulema*, and of regular
high court judges, which has the power to review large areas of legislation and to strike them down if they are "repugnant to Islam."

In 1979, the military ruler of Pakistan, General Zia-ul-Haq,
took the matter further, enacting the so-called Hudood Ordinances,
as part of a policy of increasing Islamization. Among other things,
the new laws aimed to align Pakistani practice with the general's
conception of sharia, in particular as it related to *zina* or sex outside
marriage. One effect of this was to bring into play provisions of sharia that significantly reduced existing legal protections for women.
For example, a woman who made an accusation of rape was now
required to provide four adult male witnesses to the act. If she failed
to do so, the accused must be found not guilty. However, since, in
reporting the rape, the woman had admitted to sex outside marriage, she was now liable, on the basis of her own accusation, for
the penalties of *zina*: and that meant she might be given a hundred
strokes of the lash or stoned to death for adultery.

It is important to say that, in the few cases where lower courts
have passed sentences in circumstances like these, the federal Shariat Court has reviewed them and set them aside. But there is little
doubt that the Hudood Ordinances made accusations of rape
much riskier for the women of Pakistan.

General Zia's successor, President Ghulam Ishaq Khan, moved

further with the implementation of a conception of sharia law by promulgating a *Qisas* and *Diyat* Ordinance, which replaced large parts of the criminal code that Pakistan had inherited from English common law. The effect of these changes was to treat murder and other less serious bodily harm as offenses against a person and his or her family rather than against the state. Under the ordinance, victims or their heirs were entitled to ask for *qisas*, where the offender is subjected to a harm equivalent to the harm the victim has suffered. In the case of murder, then, the heirs of the victim may ask for the death of the offender.

Now, the *Surah Al Ma'ida* of the Koran, from which this area of sharia derives, says, in verse 45:

> We ordained therein for them: "Life for life, eye for eye, nose for nose, ear for ear, tooth for tooth, and wounds equal for equal."
> But if any one remits the retaliation by way of charity, it is an act of atonement for himself.

And so the ordinance allows the victim or the heirs to waive the *qisas* and accept compensation by way of what is called *diyat*. The process by which the victim or the heirs negotiate a settlement is called "compounding."

Not everyone agrees that this is the right way to implement sharia. In particular, Pakistan's National Commission on the Status of Women (NCSW) has argued that the proper interpretation of the tradition gives the right to the *qisas* penalty not only to victims or their heirs but also to the state. If that were right, of course, then not only the family but also the government would have to waive the penalty. This would allow the state to decide to punish someone whose offense had been "compounded" by the heirs of a victim, if there was a reason of justice to do so. The members of NCSW are mindful that the victim's heirs, in cases of honor killing, are very often the perpetrators of the crime. And, indeed, in the Sarwar case, they say, Samia's brother, as heir, waived the penalty for his own parents.[26]

The *Qisas* and *Diyat* Ordinance should have led to two major improvements in the legal situation for women in Pakistan. First, it replaced an English common law tradition that had allowed for a plea of "grave and sudden provocation," which had long been interpreted in Pakistan as requiring courts to display especial leniency to those who killed in the name of honor. Unfortunately, the Supreme Court of Pakistan has declined to take notice of this change. In a 1995 decision, the Court said that the court below had been wrong to ignore the defendant's claim that the murder "was done under grave and sudden provocation as he had found the deceased in a compromising position with his wife in the early hours of morning," and ordered the murderer to be released.[27]

In a second major change, the law explicitly forbad one of the traditional forms of *diyat*, the giving of a woman from the family of the murderer as wife to a man in the family of the victim as a form of "replacement." Unfortunately, this practice seems to have continued, however, especially in rural areas away from the view of the government. Even a 2005 law that made these marriages a crime does not seem to have had a great deal of impact. These facts should remind us that changes in the law, by themselves, do little to improve the situation unless they are actually implemented: and this, of course, is not likely without changes in public attitudes. As with dueling, getting the law right is only a beginning.[28]

The most controversial cases brought under the Hudood Ordinances created an uproar inside and outside Pakistan. When, for example, Safia Bibi, a thirteen-year-old blind maid, was raped by her employer's son in the Punjab in 1983, he was acquitted because she was unable to identify him by the sharia standard; since, however, she was pregnant and unmarried, there was irrefutable evidence of *zina*. The judge ordered the pregnant girl a mere thirty lashes . . . out of compassion, he said, for her as a blind person. (In the wake of the outcry, the federal Shariat Court eventually reviewed and reversed the decision.) Naeem Shakir, a Pakistani lawyer, has rightly insisted that "Safia Bibi's case brought shame to the whole nation when the world media flashed the news" of her conviction.[29]

And that, of course, is the point. There is no doubt that a strategy we can call "collective shaming" has brought pressure on the government of Pakistan, in general, and on its political authorities, more particularly, to mitigate the more egregious abuses of women's human rights. In 2004, the Parliament of Pakistan passed a law amending the criminal code to make explicit the fact that honor killings were crimes and setting minimum sentences for such offenses. This law did not, however, alter the fact that honor killings can still be compounded by *diyat*. Then, on November 15, 2006, after many years of pressure from human rights activists at home and abroad, the Parliament of Pakistan amended the Hudood Ordinances by way of a Women's Protection Bill, which removed the requirement for four male witnesses. (Predictably, this did not please the fundamentalists.)[30]

But the same legal system regularly treats the fact that murders have taken place in the name of honor as grounds for commuting death sentences; and in many cases, honor killers or those who assist them continue to go unprosecuted.[31] In August 2008, in the remote village of Baba Kot in Balochistan, three young women who wanted to marry against the will of their families were sentenced to die by a gathering of elders. When two of their older women relatives protested, they were added to the execution list. The five bodies were thrown into an unmarked ditch. It is not certain that they were all dead when the earth was piled on their bodies.

In a scene reminiscent of the debates over Samia Sarwar nearly a decade earlier, Senator Israrullah Zehri, who represents the region, rose in Pakistan's Senate to defend these "centuries-old traditions."[32] (I am reminded of the—perhaps apocryphal—story of the British colonial official who ordered an Indian family not to allow a widow to be burned on her husband's funeral pyre. "But sir," the Indians protested, "it is our custom." "And it's our custom," the official replied, "to execute murderers.") So the combination of appeals to national honor from Pakistani human rights activists and complaints about the treatment from people outside needs to continue.

One response from within Pakistan is to complain, as that Peshawar chamber of commerce did, that people like Hina Jilani, who draw attention to these problems, are damaging the country's good name. But when a nation is doing something profoundly wrong, showing it up in the eyes of the community of nations is exactly what the patriot who cares for justice and the nation's honor *should* be doing. Beena Sarwar, the Pakistani artist, journalist, and documentary filmmaker, tells those who want the protestors to fall silent that they "need to ask themselves who is responsible: those who perpetuate the violence, or those who are its victims? What would make us a better, stronger nation: dealing with the issue, or burying it in the sand?"[33]

LIVE ISSUES

Can we learn something about the prospects for change in Pakistan from the three moral revolutions we have already explored, in which changing ideas about honor steered societies in the direction of moral progress? Dueling, Atlantic slavery, and Chinese footbinding have each been abandoned for many generations. But, as we have seen, what transpired was not so much a change in moral beliefs as a revolution—in which honor was central—in practices. It wasn't the moral arguments that were new; it was the willingness to live by them.

Of course, honor works differently in these three moral revolutions, and so we have learned that there is more than one mechanism connecting honor and moral progress. But let's begin by noticing some features that these widely disparate moral revolutions share.

First of all, the old immoral practice itself depended on a set of codes of honor. This is obvious in dueling. But remember that footbinding was an honor practice originally, guaranteeing not only the social status but also the chastity of the women of the Han elite; and recall that plantation slavery in the Atlantic world was not just an economic institution—a source of labor—but also an honor system, in which manual labor was assigned to a dishonored race, and the honor of white people, even those of the very lowest social standing, was enhanced by their identity as members of a race that could not legally be enslaved. One key element, then, in all the cases is that codes of honor had to shift if the practice was to disappear. Dueling had to cease to be a way of sustaining a claim to gentlemanly honor; footbinding had to cease to be a mark of higher standing; labor and African descent had to be dissociated from dishonor. (This last process is still underway.)

A second common feature is that the code of honor faced moral and religious challenges long before the revolution. And finally all three cases have in common that, at the end of the revolution, honor was successfully recruited to the side of morality. Dueling become ridiculous, an object of mockery, and so even a source of shame. Individuals who once would have sought honor by binding their daughters' feet now displayed it in refusing to have them bound. And Britons derived a sense of national honor from their nation's role in ending a vast tri-continental system of enforced labor.

But, as I said, the cases are importantly different, too. To see why, remember, to begin with, something I pointed out in chapter 2: identity matters to honor in two different ways. First, a code of honor shapes your options by fixing what they require a person of your identity to do. It determines a set of honor practices. And second, a code allows you to share in honor deriving from the achievements of others whose identity you share.

This second connection between identity and honor—the sharing of respect through shared identities—played no major role in the abandonment of dueling. Gentlemen in England didn't try to persuade other gentlemen to cease dueling because they thought dueling brought dishonor to all English gentlemen. The reason they changed their honor practices was that they no longer worked, in part because the honor world of mid-nineteenth-century England had been democratized and the claim of gentlemen to be entitled to this special institution now produced not respect but scorn. So they were responding to changes around them. They didn't abandon honor. They redefined their honor codes to adjust to new social conditions.

But the Chinese anti-footbinding literati did try to get their fellow literati to cease footbinding because they thought the practice brought dishonor on them all: so that is one way in which honor practices, indeed norms of many kinds, can be revised. People of a certain identity (Chinese, in this case) can decide to try and stop everyone of their own identity doing something because it brings dishonor to them all. They can also be motivated by their collective honor to want people of a different identity to stop some practice, as the British working classes wanted colonial slaveholders and the United States to abandon slavery. The anti-slavery working classes, none of whom had ever been involved in slavery, wanted these other people to end slavery because slavery itself implied a lack of respect—a source of dishonor—for them. The same democratization of culture that undermined dueling undercut slavery, too. So in these last cases it was a sense of collective honor, as Chinese or as workingmen, that helped the movements to take hold, but by two rather different mechanisms.

This is just a set of abstract historical observations. But suppose you wanted to draw lessons for honor killing, which like dueling, footbinding, and slavery is an immoral honor practice. One route to change, which we learned from the footbinding saga, meant persuading people that their honor practice brought collective dishonor on them, in the face of a wider honor world. This is the strategy of collective shaming, which we have just seen at work in

Pakistan. Collective shaming was successful not just in China but also in the first stage of British anti-slavery, when it was a middle-class patriotic movement in defense of British honor as well.

Let's recall how it works. People at home draw the attention of their countrymen to the way an honor practice harms their national reputation abroad. The strategy requires careful application because it can produce a defensive nationalist backlash, in which the practice under criticism is taken up and defended with renewed vigor precisely because uncomprehending foreigners have declared themselves against it. That is one reason why it is important that the contributions of outsiders should not be uncomprehending. Insisting that honor killing is un-Islamic—that the shame attaches not to Islam but to Pakistan and its failure to enforce the very Muslim ideals that its constitution claims are at the heart of the nation's project—is, for that reason, crucial. In the struggle against honor killing, Islam is an ally.

Honor killing is not just a problem in Pakistan, of course. It can be found in its neighbors Afghanistan and India, too. In Turkey, where the laws against it are actually enforced, it remains common, especially among the Kurds, in their enclaves within cities like Ankara and Istanbul, in those towns where they are in a majority, and in the countryside. Women are killed or scarred with acid in the Arab world—from Egypt to Saudi Arabia, from Jordan and the Palestinian territories to Iraq—in the name of honor. And they face the same threat in Iran. These are all Muslim societies where the killing is illegal, even if the law is sometimes excessively lenient when honor is offered as an excuse.

As migrants from these places settle in Europe and North America, they have brought the norms of honor killing with them;

and, as immigrant families face the challenge of adjustment to new societies with very different ideas about how young women should act and how they should be treated, the threat of honor killing has become one of the means by which fathers and brothers control daughters or sisters who resist what these men claim are the ways of their ancestral homes.

In all of these places, the challenge is to protect women from these dangers while revising the codes of honor that are the source of the threat. Not all the perpetrators of these crimes are Muslims: there have been cases among Sikhs (both in South Asia and in immigrant communities) and among Christians in Palestine. But very often they *are* Muslims: and *when* they are, we can begin the conversation by pointing out that they are contravening and dishonoring their faith.

It would be foolish, however, to ignore the fact that there are other aspects of the treatment of sexuality in law and society in a country like Pakistan that both violate human rights and have a solid foundation in Muslim traditions. Whereas with honor killing we do not have to argue against traditional Islam, there are other issues where we cannot avoid that difficulty. There are ways of interpreting the Prophet's demand that evidence of *zina* be provided by four male witnesses (or by a confession) as creating a standard of evidence so high that it will very rarely be met. And it is, I think, a plausible hypothesis that in setting these demanding standards the Prophet was trying to moderate the severer penalties of earlier Arab codes of sexual honor. After all, every chapter of the Koran save one begins by addressing God as "the most compassionate, the most merciful."

Nevertheless, Muslim societies, on the basis of unforced interpretations of passages in the Koran and the hadith, have stoned women and men to death for adultery. If an Islamic republic is to recognize the human rights of its citizens, it will have to repudiate this element of Muslim tradition. But we know that religions can find ways to do these things. The Hebrew Bible says, in Leviticus 20:10,

> And the man that committeth adultery with another man's wife, even he that committeth adultery with his neighbor's wife, the adulterer and the adulteress shall surely be put to death.

And Mosaic law, like sharia, contemplated stoning as the proper method for carrying out this sentence. But no mainstream contemporary Christian or Jewish sect wants any state to carry out this policy.[34]

CHANGING THE GROUNDS OF HONOR

Collective shaming requires a coalition of insiders and outsiders if it is to work, as we saw especially in China. In seeking to build that coalition, we can draw on the analogy with working-class anti-slavery, which mobilized a group of people by getting them to see that an honor practice in another part of the world, a practice that they themselves did not engage in, implied disrespect for them. I shall call this strategy "symbolic affiliation": you get people involved in the struggle against a practice by getting them to see it as presupposing that they themselves are dishonorable. And one of the main ways in which the outsiders have been mobilized is by way of exactly this strategy. For among the most substantial allies of those who are fighting against honor killing within Pakistan (as elsewhere) are international feminist organizations brought to the issue in large measure because they understand that the practice of *karo-kari* treats women as less worthy of respect—less honorable—than men. They care about the issue as an issue of justice, no doubt. But they are also motivated to a significant degree by the symbolic meaning of honor killing as an expression of women's subordination. It implicates, in an obvious way, the honor of women everywhere. It reflects a conviction that they are not entitled to a very basic kind of respect.

The practice of honor killing, which—despite its theoretical applicability to men—is most often carried out against women, serves not only to terrify many women into accepting marital abuse but also to provide a route by which men can rid themselves of inconvenient women with impunity. The annals of Pakistan are filled with cases where ordinary murder is disguised as honor killing.[35] A woman is therefore always open to threat from her husband, her brothers, her parents, and even her sons. Do what we want, they can say, or we will accuse you of *zina* and kill you, and we are likely to get away with it. Samia Sarwar wanted to divorce her husband—a man from whom she had parted many years before—in order to marry a man she loved. She had the right to do so under ordinary morality, Islamic law, and the laws of Pakistan. But because the divorce would have threatened the honor of her family, she was gunned down in public by a murderer brought by her mother. Worse, the fact that the family evidently connived at her death actually did salvage their honor. Though her murderer was killed in the melee after her death, there is reason to doubt that he would have been executed for murder if he had survived.[36] Politicians in the Senate of Pakistan praised her family's sense of honor, called Samia Sarwar (a married woman of twenty-nine) a *bachi*, a little girl, and described the battered women's refuge where she was staying as a "den of prostitution."[37] They sought to shame the dead woman and poured honor on her family.

Ordinary women have always worked in Pakistan, in agriculture and in domestic service. Now women of higher status are increasingly at work, too. Like Samia Sarwar and her mother, they are getting professional qualifications. They are contributing to the national economy. They are also increasingly in the habit of speaking in public and being heard. Women like the late Prime Minister Benazir Bhutto or Samia Sarwar's distinguished lawyer Hina Jilani have made their contributions to public life in Pakistan only because they were freed from a code of honor that idealizes female public invisibility. And women with these experiences will not sit silent when their sisters are murdered, as the widespread protests immediately after Samia Sarwar's killing showed. While women in rural Pakistan usually lack local organizations to support them and have few places to run to, urban women can escape to shelters like Dastak, and find the support of feminist and human rights organizations.[38] In these circumstances, the codes of honor that are used to keep women in place are increasingly under pressure.

Here we can learn from the story of the end of the duel, where an honor world was persuaded that its honor codes no longer worked. There was a revision of honor practices, from those of a military nobility to the new, more civilian codes of Newman's modern gentleman, which fitted better with the way the world now was. New conceptions of *ghairat*, which see real respect for women as central to male honor, are no doubt as hard for many

contemporary Pakistanis to imagine as a gentlemanly code organized around avoiding harm to others would have been in early
nineteenth-century England; or a marriage code that disadvan-
taged the footbound woman would have been in China in 1880.
But they are already being imagined. After Samia Sarwar's murder,
Asma Jahangir asked, "What sort of honor is it to open fire on an
unarmed woman?"[39] The slogan across the Web pages of the site
www.nohonor.org, which advertises itself with the words "Arabs
and Muslims against 'Honor' Crimes," gets it exactly right: there
is no honor in honor killing.

In all the earlier revolutions, the motivating power of honor
was channeled not challenged. The right way to proceed, it would
seem, is not to argue against honor but to work to change the
grounds of honor, to alter the codes by which it is allocated. Asma
Jahangir was asking the right question. And, as she would be the
first to insist, she is one among very many Pakistanis who have
posed it. In chapter 1, I cited William Godwin's analogous question about the duel. He asked, you will recall, whether it was not
more courageous to resist the social pressure to duel than to give
in to it. He was trying to align honor against the duel, just as
Asma Jahangir and her fellow activists are trying to align it against
karo-kari.

Violence against women is a pervasive problem across the
globe. Honor killing is only one of its many modes. But reforming
honor is relevant, I believe, to every form of gendered violence;
and, in particular, every society needs to sustain codes in which
assaulting a woman—assaulting anyone—in your own family is a
source of dishonor, a cause of shame.

HONOR AS PROBLEM AND AS SOLUTION

The three very different cases we have already considered show how changes in honor codes can reshape honor, mobilizing it in the service of the good. With the duel, the revisions in notions of gentlemanly honor in Britain in the mid-nineteenth century produced a new culture in which the central threat to gentlemanly honor—the possibility of loss of respect and shame—turned from being a reason to duel to being a consideration against dueling. In China at the turn of the last century, the honor of women of the Chinese cultural elite required them to bind their feet. Yet changes in the perception of the nation's honor among the literati led to the mobilization of one kind of honor—national honor—against the old system of aristocratic honor whose codes demanded foot-binding. Intellectuals who wanted their country to find its place in the modern world reshaped the culture of honor so that in a generation, bound feet came to be a source not of honor but of embarrassment, even of shame. In the late nineteenth century, a family of the Han Chinese elite would have had great difficulty finding a suitable husband for a girl with natural feet; by the 1930s, in most places, the opposite was true. And in finding their own honor as working people, the English working classes in the mid-nineteenth century allied themselves against the culture of slavery, which associated freedom (and whiteness) with honor and slavery (and blackness) with dishonor.

There is one other thing that is striking about each of our three examples: they were revolutions. They came, as the end of footbinding came, with astonishing speed. The movement for the abolition of the slave trade began in the decade of the 1780s and took hold in the 1790s, the two decades in which the centuries-old English slave trade reached its height.[40] In historical terms, each of these moments looks like one of those high school lab experiments, where a crystal spreads swiftly through a fluid from a tiny seed. Dueling's apogee, too, isn't far from its death knell. Looking at honor killing, a practice that is older than Islam and still pervasive in large parts of Africa and Asia, we should remember that these other ancient customs that seemed immense and enduring and immovable burned, in the end, like flash paper.

In the finale of *Sedotta e Abbandonata*, Don Vincenzo Califano collapses from the strain of organizing his reluctant younger daughter into a marriage with Peppino. As he lies dying, he makes his lawyer and his doctor promise to tell no one until the wedding is over. In the last moments of the film we see an impassive and resigned Agnese at the altar, and we see her sister, as her hair is cut off and she becomes a nun—a bride of Christ. Then, a moment later, in the final shot, we see a bust of Don Vincenzo on his grave, with the inscription: "Honor and Family." Three Ascalones have made their sacrifices to honor. But the film, however bleak, is a comedy, a satire. It was a reflection of the processes in Italian culture that made it possible for Franca Viola to resist her society's culture of honor. And the argument the film makes is not just that these practices are wrong—producing loveless marriages, thwarted dreams, suffering, even death—but that they are absurd, ridiculous; that they make Sicily a laughingstock. *Solventur risu tabulae.* The case is dismissed with laughter.

The lesson I draw is that we may have more success with the emancipation of women from honor murder in Pakistan if we work to reshape honor than we will if we simply ring the bell of morality. Shame, and sometimes even carefully calibrated ridicule, may be the tools we need. Not that appeals to morality—to justice, to human rights—are irrelevant. For the aim of anti-honor-killing activism should be to encourage more of the people of Pakistan to realize that their country is disgraced by allowing these wrongs. The wrongness of these killings is essential to the explanation of why they are shameful; as were the wrongness of footbinding and slavery to the arguments that they were sources of Chinese and British shame. And the hope I see is that when the moment comes, the change will be a revolution: a large change in a small time.

Already, as we have seen, women—and men—in Pakistan ask the question: How can a man claim to be honorable who kills a woman of his own family? Already modernizing intellectuals ask the question about honor killing that Kang Youwei asked about footbinding: How can we be respected in the world if we do this terrible thing? And they ask this question not just because their honor world has expanded to include the rest of humanity but also because they want their nation to be worthy—in their own eyes—of respect. Honor must be turned against honor killing as it was turned against dueling, against footbinding, against slavery. Keep reminding people, by all means, that honor killing is immoral, illegal, irrational, irreligious. But even the recognition of these truths, I suspect, will not by itself align what people know with what people do. Honor killing will only perish when it is seen as dishonorable.

FIVE

LESSONS AND LEGACIES

What our fathers called the archetype of honor was, in reality, only one of its forms. They gave a generic name to what was only a species. Honor is to be found therefore in democratic centuries as well as in aristocratic times. But it will not be hard to show that in the former it presents a different face.

—Alexis de Tocqueville, *Democracy in America*[1]

HONOR: THE BASICS

We have traveled through many ages and climes in search of honor's role in three past moral revolutions, visiting Wellington and Winchilsea in London, Kang Youwei in Beijing, Ben Franklin in Philadelphia, and Josiah Wedgwood in Stoke-on-Trent; and we ended in modern Pakistan where, we may hope, a revolution will soon be underway. Now we have reached the stage where, as I promised at the start, we can lay out what we have learned about honor in the form of a basic theory.

Here, then, is the picture: Having honor means being entitled to respect. As a result, if you want to know whether a society has a concern with honor, look first to see whether people there think anyone has a right to be treated with respect. The next thing to look for is whether that right to respect is granted on the basis of a set of shared norms, a code. An *honor code* says how people of certain identities can gain the right to respect, how they can lose it, and how having and losing honor changes the way they should be treated.

You can show people many kinds of respect. Every kind involves giving appropriate weight in one's dealings with people to some fact or facts about them. One sort of respect that matters involves having a *positive regard* for someone because of their success in meeting certain standards. We can term this *esteem*. We esteem people who are good at all kinds of things, from skydiving to poetry. Sometimes regard doesn't derive from success against a standard, however; and this is the second kind of respect that matters for honor. It is *recognition respect*. We owe recognition respect to police officers on duty (provided they live up to the relevant professional codes). Find a society with a code that assigns rights to respect of either kind, and you have found honor.

People like the Duke of Wellington and the Earl of Winchilsea who share both an identity and an honor world are *honor peers*. Generally, they have a right to respect from one another, which is based not on esteem but on mutual recognition of their shared status. Honor peers are equals in an important way. That kind of honor among peers is very different from *competitive honor*, which you get by excelling at something, by being better at meeting some standard than others. Achilles' honor, due to him because he was a great warrior, was competitive. Competitive honor is intrinsically hierarchical, because it ranks people against a standard.

An honor code requires specific behavior of people of certain identities: different identity, very often, different demands. Often, for example, codes make different demands of women and men. But people who respect a shared code belong to a shared honor world, whether or not they share an identity. What they have in common is that they acknowledge the demands the code makes of them in virtue of their identity and expect others to do the same. The Pashtunwali includes an elaborate code of just this kind, as did the codes that governed the Chinese literati or English gentlemen.

Both recognition respect and esteem can be distributed by honor codes without any regard for morality. The recognition respect that English gentlemen had a right to, for example, was not morally deserved. And the esteem that successful actors get reflects their meeting standards of excellence, true, but not standards of *moral* excellence. Honor codes can also require people of certain identities to do things that are actually immoral: honor killings, most obviously.

Still, one kind of honor is the right to respect you gain by doing what morality requires; and another is the kind of right to esteem you get when you do even more than morality requires. That is the honor of moral saints like Mother Teresa. Finally, morality itself requires us to recognize that every human being has, other things being equal, a fundamental right to respect that we term *dignity*. Dignity is a form of honor, too, and *its* code is part of morality.

However you come by your honor—whether by success that led to esteem, or by recognition of some salient fact about you— you can lose it if you fail to meet the code. If you adhere to an honor code, you'll not only respond with respect to those who keep it, you'll respond with contempt to those who don't. So, if you yourself meet the standards, you'll have self-respect; and if you yourself fall short, you will have contempt for yourself, which is shame. If someone doesn't feel shame when they fail (or, at least, when they fail badly) that shows they don't adhere to the code. We say that they are shameless.

What you should feel when you are keeping the code is less straightforward. Pride is shame's opposite, and you might have supposed that it is the right response to one's own honor. But some codes of honor require modesty among the honorable. Still, in many societies, honor codes invite people of certain identities to claim esteem when they deserve it and to insist upon it when it isn't offered.

Honor, we have learned, is not just an individual thing. First of all, as we've already seen, the honor code's requirements depend on your identity, which means it makes the same demands of all those who share your identity. But, second, you can share in the honor of people of your own identity, feeling self-respect or pride when they do well (and shame when they do badly) and being treated with respect or contempt by others as well. And this is so even if you yourself have done nothing at all.

A BACKWARD GLANCE

Much in this image of the life of honor sounds horribly old-fashioned, doesn't it? Nowadays we are supposed to see through such ersatz ideals and recognize that morality, properly speaking, is about the avoidance of harm, or fairness, or consent, or rights; and that your gender and your class, in any case, play no role in determining what morality demands of you. Honor is to be exiled to some philosophical St. Helena, left to contemplate its wilting epaulets and watch its once gleaming sword corrode in the salt air.

This, of course, is not my view. I want to argue in this final chapter that honor, especially when purged of its prejudices of caste and gender and the like, is peculiarly well suited to turn private moral sentiments into public norms. Its capacity to bind the private and the public together is evident in the way that it led—in Britain, in China, and now in Pakistan—from individual moral convictions to the creation of associations, and the planning of meetings, petitions, and public campaigns. All of which, as the historians and the sociologists will rightly urge, are essential to the final successes of political movements of this kind. That is one reason why we still need honor: it can help us make a better world.

But systems of honor not only help us do well by others; they can help sustain us in our pursuit of our own good. If the codes are right, an honorable life will be a life genuinely worthy of respect. Such an honor world will give respect to people and groups that deserve it. Respect will be one of the rewards of a life worth living and it will strengthen the self-respect of those who live well. In a world in which respect is given to those who live well, more people will be able to live well; the culture of respect will sustain them. So, honor is no decaying vestige of a premodern order; it is, for us, what it has always been, an engine, fueled by the dialogue between our self-conceptions and the regard of others, that can drive us to take seriously our responsibilities in a world we share. A person with integrity will care that she lives up to her ideals. If she succeeds, we may owe her our respect. But caring to do right is not the same thing as caring to be worthy of respect; it is the concern for respect that connects living well with our place in a social world. Honor takes integrity public.

THE MORAL CHALLENGE

But if moral progress is what we care about, why fuss about honor at all? We know it can go wrong as easily as it can go right, after all. It was wrong and defaming for Winchilsea to have accused Wellington of deception, honor aside. So you might think that Wellington should have asked for an apology to correct the lie, not because his honor was offended. Here, then, is the challenge that morality issues to honor: If people should do what is right because it is right—an ideal of the moral life that was first clearly articulated by Immanuel Kant—the system to which these noblemen were responding is objectionable because, even when it guides them to do what happens to be right, they will be doing it for the wrong reasons. If what's wrong is lying or refusing to give an apology you owe, why not say so? Why does it help to drag in honor?

Consider the simplest sort of case. Suppose I am someone with a sense of honor. And suppose, too, that the codes of my honor world grant a right to respect to those who deal honestly with other people, something that morality, of course, also requires. If I am tempted to lie or cheat or steal, I will have a variety of reasons for resisting the temptation. The most basic reason is just that to do so would be wrong. If I abstain for this reason, I display what Kant called a good will: I do what is right because it is right. And he thought, as he says in the first sentence of the *Groundwork of the Metaphysics of Morals*, that a good will was the only unqualifiedly good thing in the world.[2]

But because I have a sense of honor, I also want to maintain my right to be respected. So I have a further reason for abstaining, namely, to maintain my honor. I want to be worthy of respect, whether anyone does in fact respect me or not. Both duty and honor, then, provide me with reasons that have nothing to do with anyone else's actual responses to me—reasons that are, in that sense, internal. But there are also external reasons for doing what is right—reasons, like fear of punishment by the courts, that depend on what would happen if people found out that I had done something wrong. As an honorable person, I care not just to be worthy of respect but also about actually being respected; I like being respected, and besides, if people cease to respect me, they will treat me less well.

One reason Kant thought it was best if we acted out of the goodness of our wills was that if we tried to do so and succeeded, it would usually not be accidental that we did what was right. Someone who acts only out of the external concerns I just mentioned, on the other hand, will have no reason to do the right thing unless she thinks she might be discovered. Notice, though, that in the case I imagined—the case where the code honors those who do what is morally right—the concern for honor is, in this respect, like a good will. If I can get honor by doing what is morally right, then the motive of honor will be active whatever the contingencies of the external situation. So, if you valued the good will for Kant's reason, you could value honor—provided its codes associated honor with doing what was right—for exactly the same reason. Its connection with right action would not be contingent, it would be internal.

This is not, I think, Kant's own view. When he explicitly considers the "inclination towards honor" as a motive, early on in the *Groundwork*, he says that it is not worthy of the highest respect, even where it happens to coincide with the common interest and with duty. The reason is that, in his view, the only thing that deserves full respect is doing the right thing because it is the right thing to do; acting, as he sometimes puts it, from a motive of duty.

Now Kant's discussion here is of a case where honor and duty coincide "*glücklicherweise,*" that is, by a happy chance. So he isn't considering the possibility that I just canvassed of a kind of honor whose connection with morality is *not* a matter of chance. Perhaps, then, he could agree with me that, in the special case of a fully moralized honor code, which attaches respect only to doing your moral duty, honor is a motivation that is as valuable as duty. Something like this was Wilberforce's view, as we saw, and both Kant and Wilberforce were models of Protestant piety.

But Kant himself says we should "praise and encourage" righteous acts motivated by honor.[3] That seems only sensible. After all, if people find it hard (as they evidently do) to act from duty, we have cause to make sure they have other reasons for doing what is right. To meet this moral challenge, we don't need forms of honor that are fully moralized, connecting the entitlement to respect only with doing your moral duty. What we need are codes of honor that are *compatible* with morality, which is a much weaker demand. And, in fact, Kant, like the other Enlightenment thinkers I discussed in the first chapter, always writes as if honor—at least of the right sort—is a good thing.

The fact that honor can motivate good acts, however, doesn't make it a reason to do them, does it? For Kant, talk of reasons is connected to something quite grand: freedom—my self-conception as a freely acting person. Freedom is not a matter of being undetermined; it is a matter of being determined by reasons. To be free, then, is to see myself as responding to reasons for acting. Reasons are intelligible, and not just to the person in question. This is why we cannot reinterpret the reasons that guide our choices as simply reflections of what we happen to want. When, as we say, I "grasp" a reason, it makes *sense* to me as a basis for doing (or thinking or feeling) something. The reason makes me understand why I should do it. And if *you* are to make sense of me, you must grasp that it provides such a basis, too. To see your choices as flowing from bare desires is to have no real reasons at all. It's no surprise that the Latin word for the bare will—*arbitrium*—ended as our word "arbitrary."

Kant's insight was that the free will is not a will ungoverned; it is, rather, a will governed by reasons. And a will that is governed by reasons has to take those reasons as coming from outside itself.

I am arguing, against Kant, that honor is another of the calls on us made by reason; it is a call that depends on our recognition of the many different standards presupposed by those codes of honor. And when those standards make sense to us—when we inhabit the same honor world—we understand as well that those who meet them deserve our respect. Sometimes, as we have seen, the standard will be morality. Often, however, it will not.

THE HIERARCHY PROBLEM

Sometimes we are motivated by a sense of justice or by a concern to do the right thing, whether anyone else notices or not. Often, though, we are motivated (or motivated as well) by the ways we expect people to respond to what we do. People who like us, for example, will treat us better, so we want to be liked for that reason. These are what we can call "instrumental" reasons for caring about other people's attitudes to us. But by and large, we humans respond to respect and contempt not because we have instrumental reasons to do so, but because we cannot help it. It's just a fact about us that we want to be respected, and we want it, at least in part, for its own sake.

Some social psychologists have recently proposed taxonomies of the fundamental moral sentiments, the feelings that are "recruited," as they put it, by cultures to sustain their norms. The catalogue includes responses that relate to the avoidance or alleviation of harm; to fairness and reciprocity; to purity and pollution;

to boundaries between in-groups and out-groups; and to what they call "awe" and "elevation."[4] But they also acknowledge a fundamental human disposition to care about hierarchy and respect, with respect understood as something that is derivative of hierarchy. John Locke, writing in 1692, put it concisely, long ago: "Contempt, or want of due respect, discovered either in looks, words, or gesture . . . from whomsoever it comes, brings always uneasiness with it; for nobody can contentedly bear being slighted."[5] The emotions and practices of honor—esteem, contempt, respect, deference—developed, it is reasonable to suppose, with hierarchy in troops of early humans. Is honor, in this way, atavistic?

It's not a worry we can immediately dismiss. One problem with the British code of gentlemanly honor was that it distributed respect in hierarchical ways that were incompatible with morality. True, it required gentlemen to challenge other gentlemen who denied them the respect they were owed as gentlemen; but it made no such demand when your accuser was of the lower orders. The proper response, when a man of the lower orders treated you disrespectfully, it turns out, was to strike him with a horsewhip. The horsewhip was symbolic here. The distinction between knights and others in the feudal system was a distinction between those who fought on horseback and those who fought on foot. The horsewhip signified your status as a gentleman, as one who rode; the word "chivalry" comes from the French word for a knight, a *chevalier*, one who rides a *cheval*, a horse. (The highest honor in France today is still to be a Chevalier of the Legion of Honor.)

The gentlemanly code did require certain forms of behavior— duty to king and country, courtesy, and so on. But the code had regard to mere facts of birth as well as to norms of behavior: you got points by being wellborn. It continued this feature of the standard that gave Prince Hal his claims to honor. Occasionally, by the eighteenth century, it might be conceded that someone could overcome birth—that a man could be (in that condescending phrase) one of "nature's gentlemen." There was less willingness, though, to concede that a wellborn man or woman—a lady or a gentleman by birth—could be, as it were, one of nature's plebians. (Though, of course, many a young woman learned from reading novels that a member of the upper classes can behave like a brute.)

The struggle to break the tight connection between honor and birth is nearly as old as the connection itself. Recall Horace—son of a freed slave—addressing Maecenas, the richest and noblest of the private patrons of the arts in Augustan Rome, some two millennia ago. Maecenas "says it's no matter who your parents are, so long as you're worthy," but Horace complains that most Romans take the opposite view.[6] Anyone who offers himself for public office, the poet grumbles, gets asked "from what father he may be descended, whether he is dishonorable because of the obscurity of his mother."[7] This is the feature of the old system of honor that we have rejected, as we have grown suspicious of the idea that some people deserve better (or worse) treatment on account of identities they did not choose. Social status—class, if you like—should grant you no moral rights, people think; nor should your race or gender or sexual orientation.[8]

To be sure, respect isn't always connected to hierarchy. Recognition respect, remember, is treating someone in ways that are appropriate in light of facts about them, and that's often a moral duty. For instance, the moral duty to avoid causing unnecessary pain to others derives from a respect due to them because of their capacity for suffering. Even the British code of gentlemanly honor, as we saw, incorporated a form of recognition respect: within the background assumption of a shared class membership, it thus insisted on a certain form of social parity. The duel we began with brought a venerated war hero and an undistinguished peer together on a field as equals.

Yet there's no denying that appraisal respect, being comparative, does conduce to hierarchy of some sort, though we should be clear that this needn't run afoul of morality. When someone does something morally heroic, we can owe her not just normal recognition respect but appraisal respect as well, and the esteem we grant her is suffused with moral feeling. At the same time, much of the esteem we pay—much of the honoring we do—involves standards that have nothing at all to do with morality. When we honor great scholars and artists and athletes, it is not usually their moral virtues that we are assessing. (Indeed, we are by now quite used to being let down morally by our academic, artistic, political, and sports heroes.) Still, in meritocratic societies, esteem often reflects reasonable standards of evaluation. Should I not esteem a Nobel Prize laureate? Or someone my university grants an honorary degree for services to philanthropy? Or the recipient of the Légion d'honneur? Or the Congressional Medal of Honor?

"*Everybody* has won, and *all* must have prizes," the Dodo says in *Alice in Wonderland*. But we do not live in Wonderland. We can't help recognizing hierarchies in realms such as athletic or intellectual achievement: to take these realms seriously just is to recognize that you can do better and worse in them. As a result, a properly organized system of esteem can support motives that we should want to support. And since the psychological mechanisms that underlie esteem will operate whether we wish them to or not, organizing them, to the extent that we can, to align with ends we can endorse is the only sensible policy.

In response to Protestant skepticism about esteem (of the sort we saw in Wilberforce), Hume was adamant that "a desire of fame, reputation, or a character with others, is so far from being blameable that it seems inseparable from virtue, genius, capacity, and a generous or noble disposition."⁹ By "virtue" he means moral excellence, of course; but by "genius" he means excellences of other kinds. Hume's point here is the obverse of the one I cited from him in chapter 1. There his point was that you can have honor without virtue—the honor of the dueling "debauchee" is vicious; here he insists that it is hard to sustain excellence without the support its practice gains from honor. Honor isn't morality; but the psychology it mobilizes can unquestionably be put in the service of human achievement.

THE THIRST FOR BLOOD

Honor can meet the moral challenge, then, and it can also purge its dependence on morally illegitimate forms of hierarchy. But it faces a third challenge I want to consider, which is that it seems unattractively connected with violence. The duel, footbinding, slavery, honor killing: all are associated with forms of life in which honor is sustained by battle or the infliction of pain. Maybe, in the early history of our species, honor-related emotions helped give structure to groups that could hunt, protect themselves from predators, and share the task of raising children. Group action was coordinated by patterns of deference in judgment and obedience in behavior. Culture has taken these basic mechanisms and put them to other uses. But often these devices for maintaining order fail, and when they do, as likely as not, we humans, and especially we men, fight.

We are indeed a spectacularly violent species: we fight within groups, often to the point of death; and we organize ourselves to fight between groups more often than most other species as well. We fight not only for food and sex and power but also for honor. In the search for honor people spend resources, and men, more particularly, risk their lives; it would only have settled in us as a hereditary disposition if these costs once had compensating benefits. Whatever they were, they presumably explain why our concern for hierarchy—and our capacity to locate ourselves and others within it—is so well honed.

Inevitably, then, the historical changes that ended dueling, slavery, and footbinding have changed honor but not destroyed it. As we have seen, each of these changes was part of a longer, larger revolution in moral sentiments that has aimed to reduce the role of class and race and gender in shaping hierarchy. These social changes altered the meaning of honor; but they did not destroy every hierarchy since, in particular, they allow distinctions based on merit. Rather, they aimed to change the standards, adjust the criteria against which people are evaluated. But another central social project has been to tame honor's thirst for blood.

That is actually one of the striking achievements of the moral revolution that ended dueling in Britain. It removed a routine kind of appeal to violence, taming disputes about honor. (There is something of an irony here. For the duello codes had once themselves been a moralizing advance: they replaced a culture in Renaissance Italy in which young men found their honor in unregulated affrays, of the sort in which Romeo kills Tybalt in Shakespeare's play.) Cardinal Newman, in the discussion I mentioned earlier, insisted always on the gentle in gentleman—his description of the ideal, which runs for several pages, makes for fascinating reading. Not only does Newman's gentleman avoid the infliction of pain, he "has his eyes on all his company; he is tender towards the bashful, gentle towards the distant, and merciful towards the absurd; he can recollect to whom he is speaking; he guards against unseasonable allusions, or topics which may irritate; he is seldom prominent in conversation, and never wearisome."

And a little later, as if deliberately (if implicitly) rebuking the duelists of an earlier generation, the cardinal writes: "He has too much good sense to be affronted at insults, he is too well employed to remember injuries, and too indolent to bear malice."[10] From Mackenzie's and Sterne's "Man of Feeling" in the late eighteenth century to Newman's mid-Victorian gentleman there is a developing body of argument, in fiction and in the moral essay, that aims to displace the irritable masculinity of the battlefield, jealous of martial honor, with the more amiable civility of the drawing-room.

But the taming of personal gentlemanly honor did not remove the temptation to pursue collective honor with the blade and the gun. As Newman was writing, British men were going out into an expanding empire, imbued by their reading of Shakespeare's history plays or adaptations of the *Morte D'Arthur* with notions of honor more than half a millennium old. The twentieth century began with a war whose carnage was unspeakable and whose aims are impossible to remember. Rupert Brooke, a young and sensitive English

poet, who would have thought dueling ridiculous, nevertheless celebrated this pointless waste of human life with memorable vigor:

> Blow, bugles, blow! They brought us, for our dearth,
> Holiness, lacked so long, and Love, and Pain.
> Honor has come back, as a king, to earth,
> And paid his subjects with a royal wage;
> And Nobleness walks in our ways again;
> And we have come into our heritage.[11]

Those who train our armies claim that military honor is essential
in both motivating and civilizing the conduct of warfare. As I shall
argue below, I am inclined to believe them. But the trouble, of
course, is that sentiments like Rupert Brooke's—and what even
moderately sensitive soul does not feel the temptation of responding to the call of those bugles?—make us more likely to go to war.

It is no doubt utopian to hope that international society will
be able in the foreseeable future to work out ways of managing disagreement that make the threat of warfare obsolete. And if armies
are a necessary evil, the life of professional soldiers is one of the
places where we still need something close to the enduring culture
of martial honor, the honor of Prince Hal.[12] We need, though,
to keep it in its place, which is the battlefield, not the conduct of
foreign policy.

ESTEEM AND PROFESSIONAL ETHICS

As we have seen, recognition respect of a basic sort is now something we believe everyone is entitled to, in the form of human

dignity. But that doesn't mean that we won't grant different forms of respect to people of particular identities. We grant just such particular rights to respect to priests during services, managers at work, policemen in uniform, judges on the bench, and many other public officials in the conduct of their duties. Often in these cases our respect takes the form of a kind of context-bound deference: in the courthouse, we call the judge "Your Honor," and we don't criticize her with the same frankness we might display if she made a legal error in a dinner party conversation.

One of the consequences of the democratization of our culture is that we don't expect people to show deference of this sort to their fellow citizens outside the contexts of their special roles; in older, less democratic forms of social life, men could expect deference from women, the upper classes could expect it from members of the lower orders, and whites could expect it from blacks . . . and they could expect it everywhere and all the time. That created social worlds in which the experience of most positive forms of recognition was denied to large parts of the human population.

But when it comes to sustaining and disciplining those special social roles, appraisal respect—esteem—plays a critical role. It helps maintain demanding norms of behavior. As Geoffrey Brennan and Philip Pettit point out, esteem, as a way of shaping our behavior, is, in effect, policed by everybody in the honor world. The reason is simple: people in an honor world automatically regard those who meet its codes with respect and those who breach them with contempt. Because these responses are automatic, the system is, in effect, extremely cheap to maintain. It only requires us to respond in ways we are naturally inclined to respond anyway.

Suppose, instead, you wanted to achieve the same effects

through the formal mechanism of the law. Then you'd have to give new police and sentencing powers to particular people, which produces new worries. You'd face the old Latin question: *Quis custodiet ipsos custodes?* Who will guard the guards? One attractive feature of the economy of esteem is that all of us are its guards. No individual has the focused power to apply the incentives of esteem that a police officer has when she arrests you, or a judge does in deciding a sentence.[13]

Consider the code of military honor. It calls on people as soldiers (or as marines, or officers, . . . there is a variety of relevant identities) and, of course, we now know, as Americans or Englishmen or Pakistanis; and while soldiers may feel shame or pride when their regiment or their platoon does badly or well, fundamentally it matters to them that they themselves should follow the military's codes of honor.

It is worth asking why it is that honor is needed here. We could, after all, use the law all by itself to guide our armies; military discipline makes easy use of all sorts of punishments. And mercenaries can be motivated by money. So, why aren't these ordinary forms of social regulation—the market and the law—enough to manage an army, as they are enough to manage, say, such other state functions as the maintenance of the highways?

Well, first of all, both these other forms of regulation require surveillance. If we are to be able to pay you your bonus or punish you for your offenses, someone has to be able to find out what you have done. But when the battle is hardest, everything is obscured by the fog of war. If the aim of a soldier were just to get his bonus or escape the brig, he would have no incentive to behave well at the very moment when we most require it. Of course, we could devote large amounts of expensive effort to this sort of surveillance—we could equip each soldier with a device that monitored his every act—but that would have psychological and moral costs as well as significant financial ones. By contrast, honor, which is grounded in the individual soldier's own sense of honor (and that of his or her peers), can be effective without extensive surveillance; and, unlike a system of law or a market contract, anyone who is around and belongs to the honor world will be an effective enforcer of it, so that the cost of enforcement of honor is actually quite low, and, as Brennan and Pettit noticed, we won't have to worry about guarding its guardians.

There's another reason for favoring honor over law as a mechanism for motivating soldiers. The sorts of sacrifice that are most useful in warfare require people to take risks that require them to do things that are, in the jargon, supererogatory: they are acts that are morally desirable but which ask too much of us to be morally required. To punish someone for failing to do something that they have no duty to do is morally wrong. Since it is normally permissible, however, to offer a financial reward for doing what is supererogatory, that might lead you to think that the right way to regulate military behavior, if you could solve the problem of the fog of war, would be by financial incentives.

Once we have a set of shared codes about military honor, though, we also have commitments that make us think of money as the wrong idiom for rewarding military prowess: it is symbolically inappropriate. We don't give soldiers bonuses for bravery, we give them medals; and, more important, we honor them. We give them the respect we know they deserve. I have been arguing that we live not after honor but with new forms of honor. Still, our modern standing armies have kept in place a world of military honor many of whose loyalties and sentiments I suspect Wellington would have recognized; as would, indeed, Homer's Achilles or Shakespeare's Duke of Bourbon, who—realizing at Agincourt that the day is lost—cries out:

> *Shame and eternal shame, nothing but shame!*
> *Let's die in honor!* (Henry V, *Act IV, Sc. v*)

Soldiers who think like that make formidable opponents.

These reflections on why honor is such an effective and powerful way of motivating soldiers suggest that there may be analogous arguments to be made for other professions. Teachers, doctors, and bankers, for example, all do many things where it is very hard or expensive for outsiders to keep an eye on how conscientious they are being. We have every reason to hope that they will do more than can be required of them by their contracts of employment. And, as we saw in the crises in the American economy in the first decade of this millennium, the behavior of individual bankers seeking to make profits can, in the aggregate, impose large costs on all of us.[14]

I'm not an economist, and to understand how we should shape professional norms requires the sorts of reflection on the design of institutions that economists have made their professional study. But it is a noticeable fact of recent history that in many professional domains the consolations of money have, to some extent, shouldered aside those of esteem. Sometimes the two currencies have reached an unappealing compact. The surgeon Atul Gawande has argued, in reviewing the evidence about the rising costs of health care in the United States, that there are medical communities in which the values of entrepreneurship—hard work and innovation in the service of expanding profits—have overtaken the traditional guild values of the Hippocratic Oath. When this happens, esteem grows aligned with money, to the detriment, as he argues, of health.[15]

As for teaching, how often have you heard people ask what happened to the dedicated teacher who worked long hours, respected by her community and her students' parents? (Then again, if society properly esteems what good teachers do, why are they paid so stintingly?) It is, no doubt, a complex historical question both to what extent there was once a world in which in each of these professions was regulated by professional norms sustained by an honor code and how much that honor world has gone. But my suspicion, which is widely shared, is that there really has been a loss here.

HONORABLE MISSIONS

Honor, in the form of individual dignity, powers the global movement for human rights; as merited individual esteem, it allows communities both large and small to reward and encourage people who excel; as national honor, with its possibilities of pride and its risks of shame, it can motivate citizens in the unending struggle to discipline the acts of their governments. Add these to the ways in which honor can serve us in the professions. And in all these contexts it draws on a feature of our social psychologies that is, so far as we know, inescapable.

But I want to end, now, not with abstractions but with two people, a man and a woman, whose backgrounds and circumstances could not be more different. Each of them was led by a sense of honor to behave in the estimable ways that are the best argument for the life of honor. Each of them challenged a code of honor that ran against decency and justice, and in doing so moved their own societies—and not just their own societies—toward a juster future.

Let me start with the man. In early 2004, as everybody remembers, the world learned that American soldiers at the detention facility at Abu Ghraib in Iraq had abused men and women in their custody. On May 7 of that year, Secretary of Defense Donald Rumsfeld testified before the United States Senate that the guards at Abu Ghraib, like all American servicemen in Iraq, were under "instructions . . . to adhere to the Geneva Conventions."[16] This came as a surprise to Captain Ian Fishback, a twenty-six-year-old officer in the 82nd Airborne Division, who had served two tours—in Afghanistan and in Iraq—under the impression that the Geneva Conventions did not apply in those conflicts. In the course of a short career, in which he had already received two Bronze Stars for valor, he had seen detainees in Iraq being abused at Camp Mercury near Fallujah in the nine months before Rumsfeld gave his testimony. Indeed, in the course of his service in the two theaters of war he had come across "a wide range of abuses including death threats, beatings, broken bones, murder, exposure to elements, extreme forced physical exertion, hostage-taking, stripping, sleep deprivation and degrading treatment." He thought that these breaches of the Conventions might be the consequence of the fact that others, like him, were unaware of what the standards governing detainee treatment were.

And so he decided to find out what his formal obligations

actually were, not least because he had been taught at West Point that, as an officer, he should ensure that his men never faced the burden of committing a dishonorable act. He wrote later that he consulted his

> chain of command through battalion commander, multiple JAG lawyers, multiple Democrat and Republican Congressmen and their aides, the Ft. Bragg Inspector General's office, multiple government reports, the Secretary of the Army and multiple general officers, a professional interrogator at Guantanamo Bay, the deputy head of the department at West Point responsible for teaching Just War Theory and Law of Land Warfare, and numerous peers who I regard as honorable and intelligent men.[17]

None of these sources, he said, was able to provide him with the "clarification" he sought.

But talk of clarification was partly euphemism. What he had actually been doing much of the time was raising the issue of the abuse at Camp Mercury. At one point, one of his commanders suggested to him that, if he persisted in these inquiries, the "honor of his unit was at stake."[18] Captain Fishback knew, however, that there is a difference between the honor of the unit and its reputation. And so, though the U.S. Army let him down, he was not willing to give in. He provided information to Human Rights Watch investigators, telling them what he knew. When their report appeared, the Army let him down again: the CID investigators who spoke to him seemed mostly concerned to trace the names of the sergeants who had provided him with some of his information and to explore his relationship with Human Rights Watch.[19]

On September 16, 2005, Ian Fishback chose not to hide behind the anonymity he had been offered by Human Rights Watch. He wrote to Senator John McCain, urging him to "do justice to your men and women in uniform" by giving them "clear standards of conduct that reflect the ideals they risk their lives for." Eventually, Senator McCain joined two other senators in drafting legislation that did just that.

Ian Fishback shows the power of honor in the service of human decency. He understands that honor means caring not just about being esteemed but about being *worthy* of esteem, as well; and he was willing to risk the disapproval of his peers and his superiors— which is to say, the prospect of a blighted career—to preserve that entitlement. His personal sense of honor, his sense of honor as a military officer, his sense of honor as an American: all these were at stake, and at issue. "We are America," he wrote to Senator McCain, "and our actions should be held to a higher standard, the ideals expressed in documents such as the Declaration of Independence and the Constitution." Here we see the double service that a sense of national honor offers each of us: it allows us to engage with the life of our country, but it can also grant us the engagement of those of our fellow citizens who care for our common honor, too.

As for his standard of individual honor, it includes loyalty to the law and to morality as well as to the men who serve under him, and he rates these above the wishes of his superiors. Former Secretary of Defense Donald Rumsfeld—whose grasp of these truths about honor seems less certain—was quoted as saying at the time: "Either break him or destroy him. And do it quickly."[20] Perhaps he didn't say this. It is bad enough that it is so easy to believe that he did. So it is a good thing—for Captain Fishback and for his fellow citizens—that Ian Fishback is, as one of the congressional staffers who spoke to him put it, "a very powerful person," not to mention "the most honor-bound individual I've ever encountered in my life."[24]

Captain Fishback reminds us that military honor properly understood is something that all of us—soldiers and civilians—have a reason to respect. But to understand the full range of honor's power, we need to look in less obvious places than in the soldier's world. And no place could be less obvious than a farming village in the developing world. But the woman who is my second model of honor was born (about six years before Captain Fishback) in just such a place, in the village of Meerwala, near the town of Jatoi in Muzaffargarh District in the southern part of the Punjab in Pakistan. Her name is Mukhtaran Bibi, and her family farms about two acres in an area dominated by powerful members of a Baloch tribe called the Mastoi.

On June 22, 2002, her brother, Shakur, who was twelve or thirteen years old, was accused by some of the Mastois of having dishonored Salma, a woman of their tribe in her early twenties, apparently because he was talking to her in a wheat field near his home. His accusers decided to teach him a lesson: they beat and raped him and held him captive.

Shakur's father asked the local mullah to intervene, but he was unable to persuade the Mastois to relent. And so the father went to the police. By the time they appeared, the Mastois had upped the ante, accusing Shakur of raping Salma; he was delivered into the custody of the police and held in the prison in Jatoi eight miles away, charged with *zina bil jabr*, the Hudood offense that occurs when sex outside marriage involves coercion or deception.

As negotiations proceeded that afternoon between representatives of Mukhtaran and Shakur's family and the Mastois, a large group gathered in front of the walled Mastoi farmhouse, three hundred yards away from Mukhtaran Bibi's home. Mukhtaran's father, Ghulam Farid, told her in the evening that he had been assured that if he came with his daughter to apologize for Shakur's offense, the matter would be settled. And so, after nightfall, Mukhtaran, her father, her uncle, and a family friend walked toward the open space near the mosque where more than a hundred men were gathered. Mukhtaran, then about thirty years old, carried her Koran, a book she could not read but that she had learned to recite by heart, a book that she taught to the village children, a book she thought would protect her.

Five Mastoi men dominated the proceedings, waving their rifles, shouting, threatening the men who accompanied Mukhtaran Bibi. One of them, Salma's brother, Abdul Khaliq, waved a pistol. Mukhtaran Bibi laid her shawl on the ground before them, in a gesture of respect, recited a verse of the Koran, and prayed quietly to herself as she waited to see what would happen. She did not have to wait long. The Mastoi men had already decided that their response to the dishonor they claimed for the imaginary assault on Salma would be to dishonor the family of the boy they had accused. Mukhtaran Bibi was taken by four men and gang-raped for an hour in a shed not far away. When they were done, they pushed her outside, almost naked, and her father took her home.

The brazenness of the Mastoi assault reflected, of course, a conviction that they would get away with what they had done. In circumstances like these in the Punjab, a woman of Mukhtaran Bibi's background—a poor woman from a farming family—could be expected to suffer in silence; and her family, terrorized by the Mastoi, with their weapons and their connections in the police and the provincial government, would have to go along. Many women in her circumstances in the Punjab would have killed themselves.

But the next week, at Friday prayers, the mullah in his sermon condemned the Mastoi men for what they had done. The story of a woman sentenced to gang rape by a *panchayat*—a village council—appeared in a local newspaper, was taken up by human rights groups, spread by the Web, and appeared in the international press. The government of the Punjab ordered the local police to look into the matter. And so, on a Sunday eight days after her brutal assault—eight days spent in tearful isolation with her family—Mukhtaran Bibi was summoned by the police and taken to Jatoi with her father and her uncle to be questioned. Reporters gathered at the police station began to question her also and, rather than retreating in shame, she told them her story.

In the years that have followed, with the assistance of human rights activists in Pakistan and abroad, Mukhtaran Bibi has continued to fight for justice. And the authorities in her country are divided between those who help and those who hinder her cause. The local police, used to siding with the powerful, misrepresented her testimony, asking her to place her thumbprint on an empty sheet of paper and then distorting her story. But then a judge interviewed her and the mullah and actually recorded what she said. Within three months, a court sentenced six men to death for their part in her rape. But that sentence was then overruled by the high court in Lahore, which acquitted them. Then a Shariat Court overruled the high court; and the Supreme Court, faced with conflicting decisions from three different kinds of courts, intervened of its own accord and decided to consider the case itself. That was in 2005. In February 2009, there were reports in the Pakistani newspapers that the federal minister for defense production, Abdul Qayyum Khan Jatoi, who represents Mukhtaran Bibi's area in the Parliament of Pakistan, was trying to persuade her to withdraw the case. More amazing, perhaps, is the fact that the case was still pending seven years on.

In the meanwhile, Mukhtaran Bibi had been protected from her angry Mastoi neighbors by a perpetual police guard. And in March 2009, she married one of the policemen who had been sent to the village to protect her.

But while the courts of Pakistan have dithered, Mukhtaran Bibi has transformed her village and her country. The illiterate farmer's daughter has become Mukhtar Mai, Respected Elder Sister, which is the name by which she is now known around the world. When the government sent her a check for compensation, she used it not only to pay her legal expenses but also to start a girl's school in Meerwala. She didn't want another generation of the girls around her to grow up illiterate and disempowered. As her case became better and better known around the world, she received money and assistance from many places; she now runs not just two schools (one for girls, one for boys) but the Mukhtar Mai Women's Welfare Organization, which provides shelter, legal assistance, and advocacy.

Above all, she speaks out again and again about her situation and that of other rural women. Rather than hiding with the shame that her rapists meant to impose on her, she has exposed *their* depravity and insisted on justice, not only for herself but also for the women of her country. She understood that neither her caste nor her gender were reasons for denying her respect. Mukhtar Mai lives her dignity and, in doing so, teaches other women that they too have a right to respect.

Nicholas Kristof, the *New York Times* journalist who helped make Mukhtar's case known around the world, describes the scene at her home in these words:

> Desperate women from across Pakistan arrive in buses and taxis and carts, for they have heard of Mukhtar and hope that she may help. The worst cases have had their noses cut off—a common Pakistani punishment administered to women in order to shame them forever. So Mukhtar hears them out and tries to arrange doctors or lawyers or other help for them. In the meantime these women sleep with Mukhtar on the floor of her bedroom . . . every night, there are up to a dozen women, lying all over the floor, huddled against one another, comforting one another. They are victims with wrenching stories—and yet they are also symbols of hope, signs that times are changing and women are fighting back.[22]

In her own story, told to a French journalist, Mukhtar Mai describes facing the angry crowd of Mastoi men consumed with their own honor. And she writes: "But although I know my place as a member of an inferior caste, I also have a sense of honor, the honor of the Gujars. Our community of small, impoverished farmers has been here for several hundred years, and while I'm not familiar with our history in detail, I feel that it is part of me, in my blood." It is hard to know how to interpret these words, through the veil of translation. But her description of her early life and her father's response to the assault on her both suggest that she was raised within a family that understood that, wherever they stood in the local hierarchy of status, they, too, were entitled to respect.

You might ask what honor does in these stories that morality by itself does not. A grasp of morality will keep soldiers from abusing the human dignity of their prisoners. It will make them disapprove of the acts of those who don't. And it will allow women who have been vilely abused to know that their abusers deserve punishment. But it takes a sense of honor to drive a soldier beyond doing what is right and condemning what is wrong to insisting that something is done when others on his side do wicked things. It takes a sense of honor to feel implicated by the acts of others.

And it takes a sense of your own dignity to insist, against the odds, on your right to justice in a society that rarely offers it to women like you; and a sense of the dignity of all women to respond to your own brutal rape not just with indignation and a desire for revenge but with a determination to remake your country, so that its women are treated with the respect you know they deserve. To make such choices is to live a life of difficulty, even, sometimes, of danger. It is also, and not incidentally, to live a life of honor.

SOURCES and ACKNOWLEDGMENTS

These notes record my largest intellectual debts, mention some materials that an interested reader might want to pursue in thinking further about these issues, and discuss a few questions that did not find a place in the main body of the book.

I learned a great deal when I made the first version of these arguments in the Seeley Lectures at Cambridge in January 2008, and I should like to thank the members of the Faculty of History for their hospitality (and for trusting a non-historian with the past!). I learned yet more when I gave later versions as the Romanell–Phi Beta Kappa Lectures at Princeton University and the Page-Barbour Lectures at the University of Virginia in March and April 2009. My analysis of honor was the subject of fruitful conversations at the Department of Philosophy at the University of Pennsylvania in March 2009, where I gave a single lecture that focused on the philosophical argument; and at the University of Leipzig in June 2009, where I gave a slightly different lecture on the same theme. In November 2009, I gave the Leibniz Lecture of the Austrian Academy of Sciences in Vienna on honor, which afforded me more help as my work on the book was coming to a close. Equally helpful in finishing the book were the discussions on

"The Life of Honor" I had with a small seminar of Princeton undergraduates in the fall of 2009.

I don't, alas, recall exactly who said what where, but if you recognize an insight of your own from one of these occasions, I thank you for it. I am grateful, too, to all the many other people with whom I have talked about honor over the last few years. I am only sorry that I could not incorporate all their insights. Bob Weil, my editor at Norton, made many useful, detailed suggestions; both their utility and their detail are distinctive (as all who have had him as their editor know) of his work. That he is also a pleasure to work with, I had already learned in working on *Cosmopolitanism: Ethics in a World of Strangers* (New York: W. W. Norton, 2006). Finally, as always, I must thank Henry Finder for his help at every stage of the writing of this book, and especially for reading and helping to revise not one but two earlier inferior complete drafts. (He kept me company in Cambridge and in Vienna, too, which required him to hear me lecture on honor a total of four times!)

In all quotations, I have silently Americanized the spelling, where necessary, though I have kept the original spelling in the titles of books and articles. All biblical quotations are from the King James Bible. I have quoted the Koran from *The Holy Qur'an*, translated by Abdullah Yusuf Ali (London: Wordsworth Editions, 2000). Other translations, except where noted, are mine (including the rendering of Sir Thomas Malory into modern English!). I have left detailed citations in the numbered notes below. All the Web links were checked on November 27, 2009. (A file containing live links is available for download in the document library on the bottom of the Current Work page at www .appiah.net.) The book's epigraph is from Samuel Taylor Coleridge's *Biographia Literaria: Or, Biographical Sketches of My Literary Life and Opinions* (London: George Bell & Sons, 1905): 113.

PREFACE

Among the modern classics about the Scientific Revolution that I have in mind are: Paul Feyerabend, *Against Method* (Atlantic Highlands, NJ: Humanities Press, 1975); Alexandre Koyré, *From the Closed World to the Infinite Universe* (Baltimore: Johns Hopkins University Press, 1968); and Thomas Kuhn, *The Copernican Revolution: Planetary Astronomy in the Development of Western Thought* (Cambridge, MA: Harvard University Press, 1957) and *The Structure of Scientific Revolutions* (Chicago: Chicago University Press, 1962).

The distinction I draw between ethics and morality is one I learned from Ronald Dworkin, and is to be found in many places in his work. See, e.g., his *Sovereign Virtue: The Theory and Practice of Equality* (Cambridge, MA: Harvard University Press, 2002): 242–76. My own earlier work on the place of identity is to be found in Kwame Anthony Appiah, *The Ethics of Identity* (Princeton: Princeton University Press, 2005) and *Cosmopolitanism: Ethics in a World of Strangers.*

CHAPTER 1: THE DUEL DIES

I am indebted throughout this chapter to V. G. Kiernan's *The Duel in European History: Honour and the Reign of Aristocracy* (New York: Oxford University Press, 1988) for its sweeping survey of the rise and fall of the duel; and also to Stephen Darwall, who introduces the distinction between appraisal and recognition respect on which I rely in this book in his "Two Kinds of Respect," *Ethics*, 88 (1977): 36–49.

The epigraph to this chapter comes from Rule XIV of *The Irish Practice of Duelling and the Point of Honour*, which is cited in Joseph Hamilton, *The Duelling Handbook* (Mineola, NY: Dover Publications, 2007): 140 (a republication of the 1829 edition). The full sentence reads: "Seconds to be of equal rank in society with the principals whom they attend; inasmuch as a second may either choose or chance to become a principal, and equality is indispensable." For a highly influential document—*The Irish Practice* is the basis of many of the dueling codes published in early nineteenth-century America—this code has surprisingly flimsy historical sources: Joseph Hamilton quotes it from Sir Jonah Barrington's *Sketches of his Own Times* (1827) (London: Lynch Conway, 1871): 277, et seq. Barrington was impeached and removed as a judge of the High Court in Admiralty in Ireland in 1830 for embezzlement. Nor was this the only way in which he was unreliable. The Irish writer William Fitz-Patrick remarked of the *Sketches* that "however pleasant" the book was "as light reading, it is not wholly reliable as historical authority"—William J. Fitz-Patrick, *"The Sham Squire;" and the Informers of 1798 with a View of their Contemporaries*, 3rd edn. (Dublin: W. B. Kelly, 1866): 289. And Hamilton himself says, "Perhaps we should apologize for copying so many pages from Sir Jonah Barrington, who is generally considered an apocryphal authority."

The Test Act of 1678 had required members of the Lords and of the Commons to swear this oath: "I do solemnly and sincerely in the presence of God profess, testify, and declare, that I do believe that in the Sacrament of the Lord's Supper there is not any Transubstantiation of the elements of bread and wine into the Body and Blood of Christ at or after the consecration thereof by any person whatsoever: and that the invocation or adoration of the Virgin Mary or any other Saint, and the Sacrifice of the Mass, as they are now used in the Church of Rome, are superstitious and idolatrous. . . ." Similar oaths had been required in later amendments. The Catholic Relief Act abolished these oaths.

Frank Henderson Stewart's very fine book *Honor* (Chicago: University of Chicago Press, 1994) argues for the view that honor is a right to respect—see esp. chapter 2 and appendix 1. But he thinks that the sense of honor is a relatively modern development—dating perhaps, in England, to the mid-seventeenth century—and that the more central the sense of honor becomes in a society, the less tenable the whole idea of honor becomes. One reason is that having a sense of honor collapses increasingly into integrity; into something, that is, like being faithful to one's values, true to oneself. This is an important ethical ideal, one that is central to the lives of people shaped, as we moderns often are, by romantic ideas about authenticity—see Appiah, *The Ethics of Identity*, 17–21. And there is, Stewart says, no reason to pick out this one virtue from all the others and give it the special status—the organized respect—that comes with honor. A second way he thinks the growing sense of honor undermines honor itself is that the more internal we make the sense of honor, the harder it will be to know whether someone really has it. I agree with Stewart that the rise in significance of the sense of honor is an important historical process.

He also argues for a growing tendency to equate the honor code with morality, though, for reasons that should be evident, I don't believe that the equation of morality and honor is ever as complete as this might suggest. But his two arguments are meant to persuade us that once you take the sense of honor to be the heart of the matter, you will have good reason to abandon the whole system of honor. This second worry strikes me as missing a point about the sense of honor I have insisted on: which is exactly that it motivates people to act well, whether or not anyone is watching, because honorable people care about being *worthy* of respect and not just about being respected.

My response to his first worry—that there is no reason to give integrity a special place among the virtues—comes in two parts. First, in the final chapter, by showing why a sense of honor is particularly useful in certain professional contexts. But second, by insisting that honor is second-order in a particular way, even in those cases where morality sets the standard that honor sustains. Where honor's standards are moral, esteem is allocated to those who do well in some moral respect. Attention to honor in such cases just is the most basic way that we bring esteem and disesteem to bear on our moral concerns.

In Wellington's culture of honor, there were special reasons why a prime minister should not duel, one of which was that charges against your conduct in an official capacity were not matters of individual honor. So, even though he and Lord Winchilsea were in disagreement about the Catholic question, that disagreement couldn't by itself be the occasion for a duel. This didn't stop people occasionally issuing challenges against other people who attacked their character in Parliament. Daniel O'Connell—the Irish patriot whose election set the stage for the Catholic Relief Act when he was elected and then denied his seat because he wouldn't swear the Test Act oath—vowed never to fight again after killing John D'Esterre in a duel in 1815. (He also arranged an annuity to support D'Esterre's daughter.) When O'Connell referred to Lord Alvanely, in the House of Commons, as a "bloated buffoon" in 1835, the latter challenged him to a duel. O'Connell stuck by his vow, which, of course, is what a gentleman should do; his son Morgan fought the duel in his place. Morgan O'Connell and Lord Alvanely exchanged fire three times but no one was hurt. This general tendency in Britain to regard politics as an unsuitable topic for the issuing of challenges was in stark contrast with the case in the United States at the same time; see Joanne B.

Freeman, *Affairs of Honor: National Politics in the New Republic* (New Haven: Yale University Press, 2001).

The exchange of notes between the two peers and their seconds, an account of the duel by Dr. Hume, and a fascinating letter to Wellington from Jeremy Bentham about the affair, are all to be found in Arthur, Duke of Wellington, *Despatches, Correspondence, and Memoranda of Field Marshal Arthur Duke of Wellington K.G.*, edited by the Duke of Wellington (his son) (London: John Murray, 1873) Vol. V: 533–47. Dr. Hume's version of the events, written for the Duchess of Wellington, runs to several pages, and I relied upon his report for the account of the duel with which I began. Charles Greville, whose account of the response to the duel I also rely on, was a grandson both of the Duke of Portland (through his mother) and of the Earl of Warwick (through his father). He was educated at Eton and Christ Church College, Oxford, and was a pageboy at George III's coronation—Charles C. F. Greville, *The Greville Memoirs: A Journal of the Reigns of King George IV, King William IV and Queen Victoria*, edited by Henry Reeve (London: Longmans, Green, & Co, 1899).

The exchange between Boswell and Johnson about dueling bears rehearsing in full: "The subject of dueling was introduced. JOHNSON. 'There is no case in England where one or other of the combatants MUST die: if you have overcome your adversary by disarming him, that is sufficient, though you should not kill him; your honor, or the honor of your family, is restored, as much as it can be by a duel. It is cowardly to force your antagonist to renew the combat, when you know that you have the advantage of him by superior skill. You might just as well go and cut his throat while he is asleep in his bed. When a duel begins, it is supposed there may be an equality; because it is not always skill that prevails. It depends much on presence of mind; nay on accidents.

The wind may be in a man's face. He may fall. Many such things may decide the superiority. A man is sufficiently punished, by being called out, and subjected to the risk that is in a duel.' But on my suggesting that the injured person is equally subjected to risk, he fairly owned he could not explain the rationality of dueling"—James Boswell, *The Life of Samuel Johnson, LL.D. Together with the Journal of a Tour to the Hebrides*, edited by Alexander Napier (London: George Bell & Sons, 1889), Vol. V: 195.

The statistics I quote on capital punishment in England are derived from http://www.capitalpunishmentuk.org/circuits.html and http://www.capitalpunishmentuk.org/overviewt.html.

Robert Shoemaker has recently defended an alternative view of the decline of the duel as resulting from "a series of interlinked cultural changes, including an increasing intolerance of violence, new internalized understandings of elite honor, and the adoption of 'polite' and sentimental norms governing masculine conduct"—Robert B. Shoemaker, "The Taming of the Duel: Masculinity, Honour and Ritual Violence in London, 1660–1800," *The Historical Journal*, vol. 45, no. 3. (September, 2002): 525–45. He ascribes the final ending of the process to "changing judicial attitudes, a change in the law of libel, a revision of the Articles of War, and a policy of refusing to give pensions to the widows of officers killed in duels" (545). One element of this alternative story could perhaps be parsed in terms of the rise of a new gentlemanly ideal, honor as civility, which Newman represents. The new "polite" norms provide new marks of social rank. So the physical courage ideal, the premodern Nietzschean model of the nobility, declines just because every linen draper is happy to partake in it. The nobility and their new class allies have to find something else, and the Newman notion fits the bill. Not that the older ideal ever quite drops away.

CHAPTER 2: FREEING CHINESE FEET

I am very grateful to Hsueh-Yi Lin for her research support in the revision of this chapter. She was able to check passages that I had found in translation against the original Chinese, and also provided me with much useful information about China in this period. Responsibility for all the claims I make is, of course, something I must accept for myself. My own knowledge of this issue is heavily dependent on two major sources: Howard S. Levy, *Chinese Footbinding: The History of a Curious Erotic Custom* (New York: Walton Rawls, 1966); and Virginia Chiu-tin Chau, *The Anti-footbinding Movement in China (1850–1912)*, MA Thesis, Columbia University, 1966.

I refer to Chinese cities by the names we currently use for them. So, in particular, though English readers in the past would have expected Peking and Canton, I speak of Beijing and Guangzhou.

My account of Dowager Empress Cixi draws on Sterling Seagrove's *Dragon Lady* (New York: Vintage, 1992), as well as on Jonathan Spence's *The Search for Modern China* (New York: W. W. Norton, 1991) and John King Fairbank's *The Great Chinese Revolution: 1800–1985* (New York: HarperPerennial, 1987). There are two very different pictures of the role of Cixi in the period of her regency. Seagrove sees her as the passive object of the manipulations of powerful male elite figures, an unlettered and irresolute woman who occasionally acts decisively at the prompting of one or another key figure. He makes a convincing case that the original image of her as a cruel and wily autocrat obsessed with her own power is largely the product of distorted (and often simply fabricated) accounts from the turn of the twentieth century, promulgated by Chinese and foreign writers who had a variety of axes to grind. I am not in a position to adjudicate between this view and the more conventional one that ascribes many of the key moments in the politics of the period that she was empress dowager to her. But, guided by Seagrove, I have avoided ascribing to her many of the deaths that changed the balance of power around her which are part of the old legend of the Dragon Lady. Nevertheless, even on Seagrove's account, there are moments—notably at the succession crises at the death of the Xiangfeng and Tongzhi emperors and at the end of the Hundred Days—where she is the crucial figure in determining the outcome.

Seagrove places a great deal of the blame for her reputation on Kang Youwei, who wrote and said much that was highly critical of her after he went into exile at the end of the Hundred Days. Perhaps as a result of this, Seagrove goes out of his way to undermine Kang's claims to a significant role in those events. Other sources I have read are kinder to Kang. See, e.g., Luke S. Kwong's "Chinese Politics at the Crossroads: Reflections on the Hundred Days Reform of 1898," *Modern Asian Studies*, vol. 34, no. 3 (July 2000): 663–95; and Wang Juntao, "Confucian Democrats in Chinese History," in Daniel A. Bell and Hahm Chaibong, eds., *Confucianism for the Modern World* (Cambridge: Cambridge University Press, 2003): 69–89.

So the historiography of the period of the Hundred Days and of Kang's role in particular is controversial—see Young-Tsu Wong, "Revisionism Reconsidered: Kang Youwei and the Reform Movement of 1898," *Journal of Asian Studies*, vol. 51, no. 3. (August, 1992): 513–44. Wong criticizes the revisionary view of Kang's role taken by Huang Zhangjian in work published in Chinese—see *Huang Zhangjian Wuxu bianfa shi yanjiu* (*Studies in the History of 1898 Reform*) (Nangang: Zhongyang yanjiu yuan lishi yuyan yanjiu suo, 1970); *Kang Youwei wuxu zhen zouyi* (*The Authentic 1898 Memorials of Kang You-*

wei) (Taibei: Zhongyang yanjiu yuan, 1974); "Zaitan wuxu zheng-
bian" ("Discuss the 1898 Coup Again") in *Dalu zazhi*, vol. 77, no. 5
(1988): 193–99; and "Zhuozhu wuxu bianfa shi yanjiu de zai jiantao"
("Re-examination of My Study on the History of 1898 Reforms") in
Zhongyang yanjiu yuan dierjie guoji hanxue huiyi lunwenji (*Proceed-
ings of the Second International Sinological Conference Hosted by the
Academia Sinica*) (Taibei: Zhongyang yanjiu yuan, 1989): 729–68.
Some of Huang's arguments are available in English in Luke Kwong,
A Mosaic of the Hundred Days: Personalities, Politics, and Ideas of 1898
(Cambridge, MA: Council on East Asian Studies, Harvard University,
1984). I am grateful for the clarifying summary of these days in Jona-
than Spence's *Search for Modern China*, 224–30.

Second degree holders, or *juren* (which is what Kang still was
when he organized the 10,000-word petition in 1895), are also called
gongche, which literally means "public vehicle," because their trans-
portation to the capital for the *jinshi* examinations was paid for by
the imperial government. So this petition was later called the "public
vehicle petition." At least 603 *juren* signed the petition, though Kang
himself claimed (this is probably, I'm afraid, a typical exaggeration)
that it was signed by some 1,200. (Fairbank quotes a friend saying
of him: "He refuses to adapt his views to fit facts, on the contrary,
he frequently recasts facts to support his views." Fairbank, *The Great
Chinese Revolution*, 131.) For Kang's record of the "public vehicle petition" and his claims about its scale, see Kang, *Kang Nanhai zibian
nianpu* (*Chronological Autobiography of Kang Nanhai*, i.e., Kang Youwei), in Shen Yunlong, ed., *Jindai Zhongguo shiliao congkan* (*Collec-
tions of Historical Data of Modern China*), (Taibei: Wenhai chubanshe,
1966), Vol. 11: 30. See also one of his poems, which discusses this
incident, in Tang Zhijun, ed., *Kang Youwei zhenglun ji* (*Collection of*

Kang Youwei's Political Essays) (Beijing: Zhonghua, 1981), Vol. 1: 138. (Hsueh-Yi Lin, personal communication, Feb. 17, 2009.)

Though Kang was appointed to the Board of Trade after he passed the *jinshi* exams in 1895, he does not seem to have assumed his office, spending time instead teaching and publishing books and newspapers during 1895–98, mostly in Shanghai and Guangzhou—see Kang Youwei, *Kang Nanhai zibian nianpu*, 32, 37–42.

Hsueh-Yi Lin (personal communication, Feb. 17, 2009) pointed out to me, apropos of the claim that footbinding encouraged marital fidelity, that "Jonathan Spence has a good example of this in his *The Death of Woman Wang*, in which Woman Wang tried to elope with her lover but could not carry on running because of her bound feet." She also referred me, at the same time, to Li Yu's *Casual Expression of Idle Feelings*, which she describes as "a famous collection of essays on literary theories and connoisseurship in 17th century China. His discussion on women's bound feet is probably one of the most frank expressions of bound feet fetish in late imperial China. See Li Yu, *Xianqing ouji* (Taipei: Chang'an, 1990): 119–21."

It is particularly interesting that some Manchus appear to have adopted footbinding since one of the central elements of Manchu rule was a series of sumptuary laws requiring Chinese and Manchus to dress differently in order to maintain distinct identities. See Jill Condra, ed., *The Greenwood Encyclopedia of Clothing Through World History*. Vol. 2: *1501–1800* (Westport, CT: Greenwood Press, 2007): 122.

It's a measure of how many people in the mid-twentieth century believed that the need to protect the nation's honor had figured in the Chinese turn against footbinding that the Japanese sociologist Nagao Ryūzo, who worked in Shanghai for the forty years preceding the end of the Second World War, insisted to Levy in 1961 "that the Chinese relinquished the practice not because of foreign ridicule, but because of the changed mental outlook caused by the inroads of Western civilization" (Levy, *Chinese Footbinding*, 282). He clearly felt the need to insist on his alternative proposal; but, as I have argued, it is not necessary to see these explanations as alternatives.

CHAPTER 3: SUPPRESSING ATLANTIC SLAVERY

My understanding of British abolitionism is heavily indebted to Christopher Leslie Brown's marvelous *Moral Capital: Foundations of British Abolitionism* (Chapel Hill: University of North Carolina Press, 2006), which is an essential guide. I should like to mention one motive that actuated Wilberforce and his friends, which is not relevant to the argument I am making in the main text. As Brown argues, abolitionism gave the Evangelicals "a chance to win over those otherwise suspicious of campaigns against vice. Antislavery sentiment had grown fashionable by the 1780s. It had become associated with politeness, sensibility, patriotism, and a commitment to British liberty. By leading an abolition movement, the Evangelicals could draw on those more positive associations to give a benevolent, less repressive cast to their broader crusade for moral reform" (387). Of course, the Evangelicals did not make the connection between anti-slavery and patriotism, between British pride and Britain's campaign for freedom. That connection was forged in the rhetoric of the debates over American independence.

The Duke of Wellington was mocked by *The Times* in 1833 when the "noble Duke's friends" in the Lords recorded their view (in protest at the passage of the Emancipation Act) that the "experience of all times and all nations has proved that men at liberty to labor or not will not work for hire at agricultural labor in the low grounds within the tropics"—Cited by Seymour Drescher in *The Mighty Experiment: Free Labor versus Slavery in British Emancipation* (New York: Oxford University Press, 2002): 141. This was the triumph of an ideological belief in free labor over much of the evidence.

There has been much debate since E. P. Thompson's *Making of the English Working Class* (New York: Vintage, 1965) as to whether he was right to claim that by the fourth decade of the nineteenth century there really was a working class. Craig Calhoun argued in the early 1980s that the movements of the early nineteenth century reflected the dominance of artisan radicals over the new industrial workers, and were local rather than national, both claims inconsistent with the idea of a single self-conscious English working class. The radicalism of the artisans was essentially backward-looking, while the industrial workers were happy with reform; and, on his account, these decisions make perfect sense: "Communities of traditional workers had to overthrow new social relations or they themselves would cease to exist, while the 'new working class could gain an indefinite range of ameliorative reforms without fundamentally altering its collective existence'"— Calhoun, *The Question of Class Struggle: Social Foundations of Popular Radicalism During the Industrial Revolution* (Chicago: University of Chicago Press, 1982): 140, cited in Gregory Claeys, "The Triumph of Class-Conscious Reformism in British Radicalism, 1790–1860," *The Historical Journal*, vol. 26, no. 4. (December, 1983): 971–72.

Not long after Calhoun, Dorothy Thompson and Gareth Steadman Jones famously provided contesting images of Chartism—Gareth Steadman Jones, "Rethinking Chartism," in *Languages of Class: Studies in Working Class History, 1832–1982* (Cambridge: Cambridge University Press, 1984): 90–178; Dorothy Thompson, *The Chartists: Popular Politics in the Industrial Revolution* (New York: Pantheon, 1984). But despite these historiographical disputes, Miles Taylor was able to suggest, once the dust had settled, that there was a common story behind the debates between Thompson and Steadman Jones: "Chartism was predominantly a movement of the laboring poor, and was concentrated in the manufacturing districts, but was given a truly national character through its press, and its network of leaders"—Taylor, "Rethinking the Chartists: Searching for Synthesis in the Historiography of Chartism," *The Historical Journal*, vol. 39, no. 2 (June 1996): 490.

My claim that there was a good deal of frank racism in England at the time of abolition will nowadays not be controversial: one need only read Carlyle to be convinced of this. Nevertheless, it should be said that Frederick Douglass, who was quite capable of identifying racial slights, spent over a year and a half in Britain in the 1840s and denied ever being treated disrespectfully. In March 1847, he addressed a great crowd at the London Tavern in a "Farewell to the British People." "I have travelled in all parts of the country," he said, "in England, Scotland, Ireland and Wales. I have journeyed upon highways, byways, railways, and steamboats. . . . In none of these various conveyances, or in any class of society, have I found any curled lip of scorn, or an expression I could torture into a word of disrespect of me on account of my complexion; not one." (Available from the Gilder Lehrman Center for the Study of Slavery, Resistance and Abolition at Yale; http://www.yale.edu/glc/archive/1086.htm.)

Douglass's strategy, as we saw, was to enter into the battle between British and American honor, so he needed to play up the contrast between Britain and his home country in order to use the opinion of outsiders to instill in his fellow citizens a sense of the national disgrace of American slavery. It would not, therefore, have suited his argument to draw attention to British racism. But it is, in any case, undoubtedly true that his many speeches were often attended by enthusiastic working-class supporters. The rise of a widespread and more virulent anti-black racism is usually traced to the period after abolition. See Douglas A. Lorimer, *Colour, Class, and the Victorians: English Attitudes to the Negro in the Mid-Nineteenth Century* (New York: Holmes & Meier, 1978).

Sir John Seeley wrote of the British entrance into the predominant role in the Atlantic slave trade: "This simply means that we were not better in our principles in this respect than other nations and that, having now at last risen to the highest place among the trading-nations of the world and having extorted the Asiento from Spain by our military successes, we accidentally obtained the largest share in this wicked commerce"—Seeley, *The Expansion of England* (Boston: Roberts Brothers, 1883): 136. He had famously remarked in his introduction to the work that "We seem, as it were, to have conquered and peopled half the world in a fit of absence of mind" (8). So, in his view, the slave trade, like the empire, was acquired somewhat absent-mindedly. These passages and Lecky's account both show how crucial an issue it was to Englishmen in the later nineteenth century to distance their country as much as they could from the evils of the slave trade. See William Edward Hartpole Lecky, *History of European Morals from Augustus to Charlemagne*, Vol. 1, 3rd edn. rev. (New York: D. Appleton, 1921).

The suggestion that dignity is a right to respect is a standard one, but my proposal that we reserve "dignity" as the name for an entitlement to *recognition* respect is just that: a terminological proposal. I don't claim that the distinction between rights to recognition and appraisal respect is already marked in our language in exactly this way; but we do need, as I argue, to keep track of such a distinction if we are to find a place for esteem and the right to it in a democratic soci-

ety. We need it especially if we are going to resist, as I have, Peter
Berger's well-known alternative suggestion that "dignity" has replaced
"honor," the latter being a concept limited to aristocracies. See Peter
Berger, "The Obsolescence of Honor," *European Journal of Sociology*,
XI (1970): 339–47.

That the issues here are partly terminological does not mean there
is no issue of substance. I claim a place both for a competitive and
a non-competitive right to respect—for esteem as well as for dignity. Where we agree is that the association of a right to respect with
social class is normatively wrong and has been historically superseded.
Though it is worth insisting that while we do not usually publicly
acknowledge either that we *are* or that we *have* betters today, that is
surely only a polite fiction. True, only the snobbish condescend merely
on the basis of social class. But, in fact, there are many standards we
care about against which people can be appraised as more or less successful; we believe that success and failure in meeting these standards
are things we should care about; and esteem for those who do best is
an inevitable—and proper—response to that achievement.

David Brion Davis has suggested recently, in his *Inhuman Bondage,* that the abolitionist campaign reflected the shared need of skilled
workers and their employers to "dignify and even ennoble wage labor,
which for ages had been regarded with contempt"—Davis, *Inhuman
Bondage: The Rise and Fall of Slavery in the New World* (New York:
Oxford University Press, 2006): 248. The modernization of the economy necessitated a change from a society in which the lower orders
were coerced producers to one in which they were free consumers.
Sugar, coffee, cotton, tobacco, the products of plantation slavery were
the first modern consumer goods. Davis offers this proposal as a gloss
on a similar suggestion by the historian David Eltis, which he says Eltis

"unfortunately fails to develop" (*ibid.*, 247). But I wish he had done a little more to develop it himself. There is, I think, a crucial insight in the recognition that it was not just workers but their employers too who had reasons to care about the dignity of labor.

Working-class votes were less important in the context of the issue of British intervention into the Civil War than were working-class attitudes. As John Stuart Mill had written, "The motto of a Radical politician should be, Government by means of the middle for the working classes"—*The Collected Works of John Stuart Mill.* Vol. 6: *Essays on England, Ireland, and the Empire,* ed. John M. Robson (Toronto: University of Toronto Press; London: Routledge & Kegan Paul, 1982). Chapter: Reorganization of the Reform Party, 1839, http://oll.libertyfund.org/title/245/21425/736500. That was what was largely achieved by the early 1860s. It was not until the Second Reform Act of 1867 that there was an extensive working-class suffrage; and not until 1874 that the two so-called Lib-Lab members, Alexander Macdonald and Thomas Burt, both of whom had been miners, entered Parliament as workingmen.

CHAPTER 4: WARS AGAINST WOMEN

According to the *CIA World Factbook,* 42 percent of the Afghan population, or about 14.1 million people, and 15.42 percent of the Pakistani population, or 27.2 million people, are Pashtuns, and in these two countries Pasthun identity goes with speaking some dialect of Pashto. The Pashtun population of these two countries is thus more than 41 million—Afghanistan: https://www.cia.gov/library/publications/the-world-factbook/geos/countrytemplate_af.html; Pakistan: https://www.cia.gov/library/publications/the-world-factbook/geos/pk.html.

In India, people of Pashtun descent tend to be called Pathans, and it is sometimes said that there are twice as many Indian Pathans as Afghan Pashtuns. See, e.g., Shams Ur Rehman Alavi, "Indian Pathans to Broker Peace in Afghanistan," *Hindustan Times*, Dec. 11, 2008; http://www.hindustantimes.com/StoryPage/StoryPage.aspx?section Name=NLetter&id=3165e517-1e21-47a8-a46a-fc3ef957b4b1. Most of these people no longer speak Pashto, the Pashtun language, however, and in the 2001 Indian census, only about 11 million Indians claimed Pashto as their mother tongue: http://www.censusindia.gov .in/Census_Data_2001/Census_Data_Online/Language/Statement1. htm. So there are at least 52 million Pashto speakers in the world, and more than 70 million people who claim some sort of Pashtun identity. (There are also at least several hundred thousand Pashtuns in the Middle East, Europe, and North America.)

To gain a sense of the semantic range of some terms for honor in Pashto, consider these sample dictionary entries from an old Pashto-English dictionary: "*ghairat*, s.m. . . . Modesty, bashfulness, courage, honor. 2. Jealousy, enmity, emulation, a nice sense of honor." "*nang*, s.m. . . . Honor, reputation, good name, esteem. 2. Disgrace, infamy." Also in the compound "*nām-o-nang*, Honor, reputation; shame, disgrace," where *nām* means "name." From the Arabic: "*āb-rū*, s.m. . . . Honour, reputation, character, renown, good name"—Henry George Raverty, *A Dictionary of the Puk'hto, Pus'hto, or Language of the Afghans: With remarks on the originality of the language, and its affinity to other oriental tongues.* 2nd edn., with considerable additions (London: Williams & Norgate, 1867): 745, 989, 967, 4; http://dsal.uchicago.edu/ dictionaries/raverty.

The Pakistan National Commission on the Status of Women (NCSW) *Report on the Qisas and Diyat Ordinance* shows how the interaction between a variety of changes in the law has not worked to the advantage of women. This is in part the result of decisions made by judges in interpreting the law. Thus, the ordinance allows the judge to give a sentence at his or her discretion, even if the heirs agree to accept *diyat*, but this appears almost never to occur in cases of honor killing. The general impression you get from reading the report is that some in the legal system share the attitudes of the many senators who declined to support the motion criticizing the murder of Samia Sarwar. (The NCSW *Report on the Qisas and Diyat Ordinance*, 1990, can be retrieved from the UN Secretary-General's Database on Violence Against Women at http://webapps01.un.org/vawdatabase/searchDetail.action?measure Id=18083&baseHREF=country&baseHREFId=997.)

CHAPTER 5: LESSONS AND LEGACIES

The best recent book on the social workings of esteem is Geoffrey Brennan and Philip Pettit, *The Economy of Esteem* (New York: Oxford University Press, 2005), which I have found extremely helpful. Their book is about esteem, not about the right to esteem, and their aim is to explore the structuring of institutions for its distribution, so their focus is different from—indeed, complementary to—mine.

For recent work on the basic psychological processes "recruited" by the cultural systems of morality, see Jonathan Haidt and Craig Joseph, "Intuitive Ethics: How innately prepared intuitions generate culturally variable virtues," *Daedalus* (Fall 2004): 55–66; and Jonathan Haidt and Fredrik Björklund, "Social Intuitionists Answer Six Questions About Moral Psychology," in Walter Sinnott-Armstrong, ed., *Moral Psychology*, Vol. 2: *The Cognitive Science of Morality: Intuition and Diversity* (Cambridge, MA: MIT Press, 2008): 181–218. Among the works they surveyed in identifying cross-cultural regularities were Donald Brown, *Human Universals* (Philadelphia: Temple University Press, 1991); Franz de Waal, *Good Natured: The Origins of Right and Wrong in Humans and Other Animals* (Cambridge, MA: Harvard University Press, 1996); S. H. Schwartz and W. Bilsky, "Toward a Theory of the Universal Content and Structure of Values: Extensions and cross-cultural replications," *Journal of Personality and Social Psychology,* 58 (1990): 878–91; and the influential "three ethics" proposal elaborated in Richard Shweder *et al.*, "The 'Big Three' of Morality (Autonomy, Community, and Divinity), and the 'Big Three' Explanations of Suffering," in A. Brandt and Paul Rozin (eds.), *Morality and Health* (New York: Routledge, 1997): 119–69.

My account of Mukhtaran Bibi's experience is based mostly on her own autobiography, published under the name by which she is now known, Mukhtar Mai, with the title *In the Name of Honor: A Memoir* (New York: Atria Books, 2006). This is an "as told to" memoir, originally written in French by Marie-Thérèse Cuny, who had the service of two translators from Saraiki, the language of Meerwala. Nicholas Kristof and Sheryl WuDunn have an engaging and engaged account of Mukhtar Mai in *Half the Sky: Turning Oppression into Opportunity for Women Worldwide* (New York: Random House, 2009). The accounts of June 22, 2002, available from many sources in newspapers and on the Web are divergent in detail. But the basic facts are not in serious dispute.

NOTES

PREFACE

1. René Descartes, "Comments on a Certain Broadsheet" (1648), in *The Philosophical Writings of Descartes*. Vol. 1, trans. John Cottingham, Robert Stoothoff, and Dugald Murdoch (Cambridge: Cambridge University Press, 1987): 307.

CHAPTER 1: THE DUEL DIES

1. Christopher Hibbert, *Wellington: A Personal History* (Reading, MA: Perseus/HarperCollins, 1999): 275.
2. Wellington, *Despatches, Correspondence, and Memoranda*, V: 542.
3. Joseph Hendershot Park, ed., *British Prime Ministers of the Nineteenth Century: Policies and Speeches* (Manchester, NH: Ayer Publishing, 1970): 62.
4. Wellington, *Despatches*, V: 527.
5. Greville, *Memoirs*, 250.
6. A copy of the note, from the archives of King's College London, is at http://www.kcl.ac.uk/depsta/iss/archives/wellington/duel08a.htm.
7. Sir William Blackstone, *Commentaries on the Laws of England* (Oxford: Clarendon Press, 1765–69), Bk IV, chapter 14, "Of Homicide"; http://avalon.law.yale.edu/18th_century/blackstone_bk4ch14.asp.

8. Sir Algernon West, *Recollections: 1832–1886* (New York & London: Harper & Bros., 1900): 27.

9. Sir Thomas Malory, *Le Morte Darthur the original edition of William Caxton now reprinted and edited with an introduction and glossary by H. Oskar Sommer; with an essay on Malory's prose style by Andrew Lang* (Ann Arbor: University of Michigan Humanities Text Initiative, 1997): 291; http://name.umdl.umich.edu/MaloryWks2.

10. Stewart, *Honor*, 44–47.

11. Hugh Lloyd-Jones, "Honor and Shame in Ancient Greek Culture," in *Greek Comedy, Hellenistic Literature, Greek Religions, and Miscellanea: The Academic Papers of Sir Hugh Lloyd-Jones* (Oxford: Clarendon Press, 1990): 279.

12. For Asante in the nineteenth century, see John Iliffe, *Honor in African History* (Cambridge: Cambridge University Press, 2004): 83–91.

13. Homer, *The Iliad*, trans. Robert Fagles (New York: Viking Penguin, 1990): 523.

14. Kiernan, *The Duel in European History*, 216.

15. *Ibid.*, 102.

16. *Ibid.*, 190.

17. Hamilton, *The Duelling Handbook*, 138. (quoted slightly differently in Robert Baldick, *The Duel: A History of Duelling* [London: Hamlyn, 1970]: 33–34). Cited in Douglass H. Yarn, "The Attorney as Duelist's Friend: Lessons from The Code Duello," 51, *Case W. Res. L. Rev.*, 69 (2000): 75–76, n. 71.

18. Wellington, *Despatches*, V: 539.

19. Tresham Lever, *The Letters of Lady Palmerston: Selected and Edited from the Originals at Broadlands and Elsewhere* (London: John Murray, 1957): 118.

20. Frances Shelley, *The Diary of Frances Lady Shelley*, ed. R. Edgecumbe (London: John Murray, 1913): 74.

21. Hamilton, *The Duelling Handbook*, 140.

22. Wellington, *Despatches*, V: 539.

23. *Ibid.*, V: 544.

24. Lord Broughton (John Cam Hobhouse), *Recollections of a Long Life with Additional Extracts from His Private Diaries*, ed. Lady Dorchester. Vol. 3: *1822–1829* (New York: Charles Scribner's Sons, 1910): 312–13.

25. V. Cathrein, "Duel," in *The Catholic Encyclopedia*, Vol. 5 (New York: Robert Appleton Company, 1909); http://www.newadvent.org/cathen/05184b.htm.

26. Council of Trent, 25th Session, Dec. 3 and 4, 1563, "On Reformation," chapter 19. Available at http://www.intratext.com/IXT/ENG0432/_P2J.HTM.

27. Francis Bacon, *The Letters and the Life of Francis Bacon, Vol. 4*, ed. James Spedding (London: Longmans, Green, Reader & Dyer, 1868): 400.

28. Edward Herbert, *The Autobiography of Edward, Lord Herbert of Cherbury*, ed. Will H. Dircks (London: Walter Scott, 1888): 22.

29. Amelot de Houssaye, cited in Charles Mackay, *Memoirs of Extraordinary Popular Delusions and the Madness of Crowds* (Ware, Herts: Wordsworth Editions, 1995): 668.

30. Bacon, *Letters and Life*, 400. Those "pamphlets" are the duello codes.

31. This is John Chamberlain's description of the situation in the letter of 1613 in which he lists the disputes just mentioned. Spedding (ed.) cites it in Bacon, *op. cit.*, 396.

32. Bacon, *op. cit.*, 409, 399.

33. William Hazlitt, *The Complete Works of William Hazlitt*, ed. P. P. Howe (London & Toronto: J. M. Dent & Sons, 1934), Vol. 19: 368.

34. Jeremy Bentham, *An Introduction to the Principles of Morals and Legislation* (1823) (Oxford: Clarendon Press, 1907), chapter 13, para. 2; http://www.econlib.org/library/Bentham/bnthPML13.html#Chapter%20XIII,%20Cases%20Unmeet%20for%20Punishment.

35. William Robertson, *The History of the Reign of the Emperor Charles V* (New York: Harper & Bros., 1836): 225.

36. David Hume, *Essays, Moral, Political, and Literary*. Library of Economics and Liberty, at http://www.econlib.org/library/LFBooks/Hume/hmMPL50.html.

37. Francis Hutcheson, *Philosophiae moralis institutio compendiaria with A Short Introduction to Moral Philosophy*, ed. Luigi Turco (Indianapolis: Liberty Fund, 2007). Chapter XV: Of Rights Arising from Damage Done, and the Rights of War, http://oll.libertyfund.org/title/2059.

38. Hamilton, *The Duelling Handbook*, 125.

39. Adam Smith, *Lectures on Jurisprudence*, ed. R. L. Meek, D. D. Raphael, and P. G. Stein. Vol. 5 of the Glasgow Edition of the *Works and Correspondence of Adam Smith* (Indianapolis: Liberty Fund, 1982). Chapter: Friday, January 21st, 1763; http://oll.libertyfund.org/title/196.

40. William Godwin, *An Enquiry Concerning Political Justice, and its Influence on General Virtue and Happiness,* Vol. 1 (London: G. G. J. & J. Robinson, 1793). Chapter: Appendix, No. II: Of Duelling; http://oll.libertyfund. org/title/90/40264.

41. Boswell, *The Life of Samuel Johnson, LL.D. Together with the Journal of a Tour to the Hebrides*, ed. Napier, V: 195.

42. Voltaire, *Dictionnaire Philosophique, Oeuvres Complètes de Voltaire* (Paris: De l'Imprimerie de la Société Litteraire-Typographique, 1784), Vol. 36: 400.

43. David Hume, *The History of England from the Invasion of Julius Caesar to the Revolution in 1688* (1778), 6 vols. (Indianapolis: Liberty Fund, 1983), Vol. 3: 169.

44. Boswell, *op. cit.*, 2: 343.

45. From the account offered by King's College London at http://www.kcl. ac.uk/depsta/iss/archives/wellington/duel12.htm.

46. This cartoon is available, with another better known one of the event by William Heath, on the Web site of King's College London at http://www .kcl.ac.uk/depsta/iss/archives/wellington/duel16.htm.

47. I am very grateful to Philip Pettit for this suggestion.

48. Greville, *Memoirs*, 196.

49. *Ibid.*, 198.

50. *Ibid.*, 199.

51. Hibbert, *Wellington: A Personal History*, 275. The *Literary Gazette* is cited by Hamilton (*op. cit.*, xiv).

52. http://www.kcl.ac.uk/depsta/iss/archives/wellington/duel12.htm.

53. Duke of Wellington, *Despatches,* V: 585.

54. Bacon, *op. cit.*, 400.

55. Richard Cobden, *Speeches on Questions of Public Policy by Richard Cobden M.P.*, ed. John Bright and James E. Thorold Rogers (London: Macmillan & Co., 1878): 565.

56. Mill, *Collected Works of John Stuart Mill*. Vol. 18: *Essays on Politics and*

Society Part I, ed. John M. Robson (Toronto: University of Toronto Press; London: Routledge & Kegan Paul, 1977). Chapter: De Tocqueville on Democracy in America [II], 1840, http://oll.libertyfund.org/title/233/16544/799649.

57. Lord Broughton, *op. cit.*, 312.

58. John Henry Cardinal Newman, *The Idea of a University* (London: Longmans, Green & Co., 1919): 208.

59. James Kelly, *That Damn'd Thing Called Honour: Duelling in Ireland 1570–1860* (Cork: Cork University Press, 1995): 267.

60. James Landale, *The Last Duel: A True Story of Death and Honour* (Edinburgh: Canongate, 2005).

61. Kiernan, *The Duel in European History*, 218, says that this "has been called the last duel in England." He makes his case less plausible by putting the affair three years too early, in 1849.

62. Sir Algernon West, *Recollections*, 28, quoting Horace, *Satires*, Bk 2, 1. Line 86 is "Solventur risu tabulae, tu missus abibis," (I've corrected Sir Algernon's "solvuntur," though it is often misquoted that way)—"The charges will be dismissed with laughter; released, you will leave." Horace is pointing out that a libel action—*tabulae* are the elements laid before a judge—will be dismissed with laughter if the scandalous verses complained of are funny enough.

63. Sir William Gregory, *An Autobiography*, ed. Lady Gregory (London: John Murray, 1894): 149–51.

64. Evelyn Waugh, *The Sword of Honour Trilogy* (New York: Knopf, 1994): 449.

CHAPTER 2: FREEING CHINESE FEET

1. Quoted in Howard S. Levy, *Chinese Footbinding: The History of a Curious Erotic Custom* (New York: Walton Rawls, 1966): 72.

2. Robert Hart, *The I.G. in Peking: Letters of Robert Hart, Chinese Maritime Customs (1868–1907)*, ed. John King Fairbank, Katherine Frost Brunner, and Elizabeth MacLeod Matheson (Cambridge, MA: Harvard University Press, 1976) Vol. 2: 1311.

3. Keith Laidler, *The Last Empress: The She-Dragon of China* (Chichester: John Wiley & Sons, 2003): 32.

4. Timothy Richard, *Forty-five Years in China* (New York: Frederick A. Stokes Company, 1916): 253, et seq.

5. John King Fairbank and Merle Goldman, *China: A New History* (Cambridge, MA: Harvard University Press, 2006): 229.

6. Richard, *op. cit.*, 262.

7. Weng Tonghe: tutor of Tongzhi (r. 1861–75) and Guangxu emperors. Kang's friendship with Weng Tonghe dated back to 1895. See Kang, *Kang Nanhai zibian nianpu*, 33–37 (Hsueh-Yi Lin, personal communication, Feb. 17, 2009).

8. Yong Z. Volz, "Going Public Through Writing: Women Journalists and Gendered Journalistic Space in China, 1890s–1920s," *Media Culture Society*, vol., 29, no. 3 (2007): 469–89.

9. Levy, *op. cit.*, 72.

10. *Ibid.* I have amended and extended Levy's translation here on the basis of Hsueh-Yi Lin's translation of the original. Kang Youwei, "Qing jin funü guozu zhe" ("Memorial Pleading to Ban the Footbinding of Women"), in Tang Zhijun, ed., *Kang Youwei zhenglun ji* (Beijing: Zhonghua, 1981): 335. She also informs me that the last sentence here is "a common rhetorical device in a memorial" (Personal communication, Feb. 17, 2009).

11. Brennan and Pettit, *The Economy of Esteem*, 19.

12. Levy *op. cit.*, 39.

13. *Ibid.*

14. Mrs. Archibald Little, *The Land of the Blue Gown* (London: T. Fisher & Unwin, 1902): 363.

15. Gerry Mackie, "Ending Footbinding and Infibulation: A Convention Account," *American Sociological Review*, vol. 61, no. 6 (December, 1996): 1008.

16. Lanling Xiaoxiao Sheng, *The Golden Lotus*, trans. Clement Egerton Vol 1: 101 (my edition has the publication details in Chinese). Levy (*op. cit.*, 51) expresses some doubts as to the reliability of Egerton's translation.

17. Levy, *op. cit.*, 55.

18. *Ibid.*, 60.

19. Chau, MA Thesis, 13–16.

20. Levy, *op. cit.*, 283–84.

21. *Ibid.*, 107.

22. *Ibid.*, 65, 248, 118.

23. Endymion Wilkinson, *Chinese History: A Manual*, rev. edn. (Cambridge, MA: Harvard University Press, 2000): 273–77. The emperor's reign officially ended in 1795, after sixty years on the throne, apparently because piety required him not to rule longer than his predecessor; but he continued as regent until his death in 1799.

24. Patricia Buckley Ebrey, *Cambridge Illustrated History of China* (Cambridge: Cambridge University Press, 1996): 199.

25. Kwang-Ching Liu, Foreword, in *ibid.*, 6.

26. *Ibid.*, 229.

27. Harley Farnsworth MacNair, *Modern Chinese History: Selected Readings* (Shanghai: Commercial Press Ltd., 1923): 2, 4.

28. Arthur Waley, *The Opium War Through Chinese Eyes* (Stanford: Stanford University Press, 1958): 103.

29. Fairbank and Goldman, *op. cit.*, 222.

30. Arthur P. Wolf and Chuang Ying-Chang, "Fertility and Women's Labour: Two Negative (But Instructive) Findings," *Population Studies*, vol. 48, no. 3 (November 1994): 427–33.

31. Hsueh-Yi Lin, personal communication, June 10, 2009.

32. Fairbank and Goldman, *op. cit.*, 218.

33. Chau, *op. cit.*, 19, 20.

34. *Ibid.*, 22.

35. *Ibid.*, 23. Li Ju-Chen (Li Ruzhen), *Flowers in the Mirror*, trans. and ed. Lin Tai-Yi (Berkeley and Los Angeles: University of California Press, 1965): 113.

36. Mrs. Archibald Little, *Intimate China*, cited in Chau, *op. cit.*, 41.

37. Dorothy Ko, *Cinderella's Sisters: A Revisionist History of Footbinding* (Berkeley: University of California Press, 2005): 15.

38. Chau, *op. cit.*, 45, 57.

39. Ko, *op. cit.*, 16.
40. Fan Hong, *Footbinding, Feminism and Freedom: The Liberation of Women's Bodies in Modern China* (London: Cass, 1997).
41. Patrick Hanan, "The Missionary Novels of Nineteenth-Century China," *Harvard Journal of Asiatic Studies*, vol. 60, no. 2 (December 2000): 440. Chau *op. cit.*, 28.
42. Richard, *Forty-five Years in China*, 158.
43. *Ecumenical Mission Conference New York, 1900* (New York: American Tract Society; London: Religious Tract Society, 1900), Vol. 1: 552.
44. Fairbank and Goldman, *op. cit.*, 222.
45. Chau, *op. cit.*, 51.
46. Levy, *op. cit.*, 74.
47. Angela Zito, "Secularizing the Pain of Footbinding in China: Missionary and Medical Stagings of the Universal Body," *Journal of the American Academy of Religion*, vol. 75, no. 1 (March 2007): 4–5.
48. See "Mrs. Archibald Little, About the Author"; http://www.readaround asia.co.uk/miclittle.html.
49. Fan Hong, *op. cit.*, 57.
50. Little, *The Land of the Blue Gown*, 306–09.
51. Richard, *Forty-five Years in China*, 227–28.
52. Yen-P'ing Hao and Erh-Min Wang, "Changing Chinese Views of Western Relations, 1840–95," in *Cambridge History of Modern China. Vol. 2: The Late Ch'ing 1800–1911*, Part II, ed. Denis Crispin Twitchett and John King Fairbank (Cambridge: Cambridge University Press, 1978): 201.
53. Richard, *Forty-five Years in China*, 265–67.
54. Fairbank and Goldman, *op. cit.*, 231.
55. See the discussion of this period in Seagrove's *Dragon Lady* and also Hens van de Ven, "Robert Hart and Gustav Detring During the Boxer Rebellion," *Modern Asian Studies*, vol. 40, no. 3 (2006): 631–62.
56. Chau, *op. cit.* 121, citing the contemporaneous translation in the *North Chinese Herald*.
57. Levy, *op. cit.*, 278–79.
58. Fan Hong, *op. cit.*, chapters 3 and 4.

59. Chau, *op. cit.*, 104.

60. Cited in *ibid.*, 98.

61. Levy, *op. cit.*, 128, 181, 94.

62. J. M. Coetzee, "On National Shame," *Diary of a Bad Year* (New York: Viking, 2007): 39, 45. This is a novel that reproduces essays written by the protagonist.

63. This is one of the central ideas of Benedict Anderson's *Imagined Communities: Reflections on the Origin and Spread of Nationalism* (London & New York: Verso, 2006).

64. Ernest Renan, *Qu'est-ce qu'une nation?* 2nd edn. (Paris: Calmann-Lévy, 1882): 26.

65. Mackie, *op. cit.*, 1001.

66. Levy, *op. cit.*, 171.

CHAPTER 3: SUPRESSING ATLANTIC SLAVERY

1. Lecky, *History of European Morals*, Vol. 1. Chapter 1: The Natural History of Morals; http://oll.libertyfund.org/title/1839/104744/2224856.

2. Eric Williams, *Capitalism and Slavery* (Chapel Hill: University of North Carolina Press, 1994): 142, 210–11.

3. *Ibid.*, 211.

4. Drescher, *Capitalism and Antislavery*, 5.

5. *Ibid.*, 7.

6. *Ibid.*, 11, citing work by Wrigley and Schofield.

7. Benjamin Disraeli, *Lord George Bentinck: A Political Biography* (London: G. Routledge & Co., 1858): 234.

8. The passage continues: "This was also a Roman characteristic—especially that of Marcus Aurelius," and then ends with the sentence I cited above.

9. *Encyclopédie, ou Dictionnaire raisonné des sciences, des arts et des métiers, par une société de gens de lettres.* Mis en ordre & publié par M. Diderot . . . & quant a la partie mathématique, par M. d'Alembert, 28 vols. (Geneva Paris & Neufchastel, 1772; 1754–72). Cited from *The Making of the Modern World* (Farmington Hills, MI: Thomson Gale. 2007), Vol. 16: 532.

10. The "him" here is "conscience." Erasmus Darwin, "The Loves of the

Plants" (1789) in *The Botanic Garden* (London: Jones & Company, 1825): 173.

11. Erasmus Darwin, *Zoonomia; or, The Laws of Organic Life* (Philadelphia: Edward Earle, 1818), Vol. 2: 325.

12. As Thomas Carlyle put it derisively in *Past and Present*, "Methodism with its eye forever turned on its own navel: asking itself with torturing anxiety of Hope and Fear, 'Am I right? Am I wrong? Shall I be saved? shall I not be damned?'—what is this at bottom, but a new phase of Egoism, stretched out into the Infinite; not always the heavenlier for its infinitude"—Carlyle, *Past and Present* (1843) (London: Chapman & Hall, 1872): 101.

13. David Turley, *The Culture of English Antislavery, 1780–1860* (London: Routledge, 1991): 9.

14. Brown, *Human Universals*, 391.

15. *Ibid.*, 429.

16. It's perhaps important to add that the Society's leadership contained many Quakers as well.

17. Drescher, *op. cit.*, 28–29.

18. David Brion Davis, *The Problem of Slavery in the Age of Revolution: 1770–1823* (Ithaca: Cornell University Press, 1975): 435.

19. Brown, *op. cit.*, 437.

20. Laurence Sterne, *A Sentimental Journey* (1768) (London: Penguin Books, 2001): 69–70.

21. William Cowper's "The Negro's Complaint," *The Gentleman's Magazine* (December 1793), ll. 55–56, in *The Complete Poetical Works of William Cowper*, ed. H. S. Milford (London: Henry Frowde, 1905), 371–72.

22. Cited in Brown, *op. cit.*, 166.

23. Cited in *ibid.*, 71, 141–42.

24. *Ibid.*, 371.

25. *Ibid.*, 134.

26. Cited in *ibid.*, 170.

27. Frederick Douglass, *The Life and Writings of Frederick Douglass* (New York: International Publishers, 1950), Vol. 1: 147.

28. The repressions of the late eighteenth century also suppressed many of

the radical organizations that supported abolition—see Thompson *The Making of the English Working Class*.

29. William Wilberforce, *An Appeal to the Religion, Justice, and Humanity of the Inhabitants of the British Empire in Behalf of the Negro Slaves in the West Indies* (London: J. Hatchard & Son, 1823): 1.

30. William Wilberforce, *A Practical View of the Prevailing Religious System of Professed Christians, in the Higher and Middle Classes in This Country Contrasted with Real Christianity* (New York: American Tract Society, 1830): 241, 249–50 (first published in England in 1797).

31. *Ibid.*, 105.

32. Williams, *op. cit.*, 181.

33. *Letters on the Necessity of a Prompt Extinction of British Colonial Slavery; Chiefly Addressed to the More Influential Classes* (Leicester: Thomas Combe & Son, 1826): 104.

34. *Ibid.*, 149, 163, 165, 184, 159.

35. Disraeli, *Lord George Bentinck*, 234.

36. "London Workingmen's Association: Further Papers," in *London Radicalism 1830–1843: A selection of the Papers of Francis Place*, ed. D. J. Rowe (London: London Record Society, 1970): 160–77; http://www.british-history.ac.uk/source.aspx?pubid=230.

37. Betty Fladeland, *Abolitionists and Working-Class Problems in the Age of Industrialization* (London: Macmillan, 1984).

38. Thompson, *op. cit.*, 807.

39. See Orlando Patterson, *Slavery and Social Death* (Cambridge, MA: Harvard University Press, 1985).

40. William Cobbett, *Rural Rides* (1830) (London: J. M. Dent & Sons, 1912): 306–07.

41. Catherine Gallagher, *The Industrial Reformation of English Fiction* (Chicago: University of Chicago Press, 1988): 10. The second passage she quotes from Cobbett's *Weekly Political Register*, 7 (1805): 372.

42. Ibid., citing Cobbett's *Weekly Political Register*, 7 (1806): 845.

43. Ibid., 9, citing Cobbett's *Weekly Political Register*, August 27, 1823.

44. *Universal Declaration of Human Rights*; http://www.un.org/en/documents/udhr/.

45. Samuel Johnson LL. D., *A Dictionary of the English Language*, ed. John Walker and R. S. Jameson, 2nd edn. (London: William Pickering Chancery Lane; George Cowie & Co. Poultry Lane, 1828): 204. The same dictionary defines "dignify" as "To advance; to prefer; to exalt; to honor; to adorn; to give luster to," reminding us of the close association between honor and dignity.

46. Edmund Burke, *Reflections on the Revolution in France* (1790) (New York: Oxford University Press, 1999): 49.

47. Thomas Hobbes, *Hobbes's Leviathan reprinted from the edition of 1651 with an Essay by the Late W. G. Pogson Smith* (Oxford: Clarendon Press, 1909). Chap. XVII: Of the Causes, Generation, and Definition of a Common-Wealth, http://oll.libertyfund.org/title/869/208775/3397532.

48. For many people in the Abrahamic religions, of course, one of the grounds of our dignity is that we are all created "in God's image."

49. Seymour Drescher, "Public Opinion and the Destruction of British Colonial Slavery," in James Walvin, ed., *Slavery and British Society 1776–1848* (Baton Rouge: Louisiana State University Press, 1982): 29.

50. James Walvin, "The Propaganda of Anti-Slavery," in Walvin, ed., *op. cit.*, 52–53, 54.

51. *Ibid.*, 53. For the statistics, see *ibid.*, 54–55.

52. Cited in Alan Nevins, *The War for the Union. Vol. 2: War Becomes Revolution: 1862–1863* (New York: Charles Scribner's Sons, 1960): 244.

53. *Ibid.*, 250.

54. "In May 1847, Dr. Bowring chaired the first annual meeting of the debt-ridden and moribund league. That meeting was also its last"—Douglas C. Stange, *British Unitarians Against American Slavery, 1833–65* (Rutherford, NJ: Fairleigh Dickinson University Press, 1984): 88.

55. For Sir Henry Molesworth's comment, see the article on Vincent in Sidney Lee, ed., *Dictionary of National Biography* (London: Smith, Elder, & Co., 1909), Vol. 20: 358. The comment on missed opportunities is from William McFeely, *Frederick Douglass* (New York: W. W. Norton, 1995): 138–39.

CHAPTER 4: WARS AGAINST WOMEN

1. Quoted in Richard Galpin "Woman's 'Honour' Killing Draws Protests in Pakistan," *The Guardian* (London), April 8, 1999; http://www.guardian.co.uk/world/1999/apr/08/14.

2. *Sedotta e Abbandonata* (*Seduced and Abandoned*) (1964), Pietro Germi, director; story and screenplay by Luciano Vincenzoni.

3. John Webber Cook, *Morality and Cultural Differences* (New York: Oxford University Press, 1999): 35.

4. Melodia was murdered in 1978 in a Mafia-style execution two years after being released from jail.

5. "Il consiglio che voglio dare è di stare sempre attenti, ma di prendere ogni decisione seguendo sempre il proprio cuore"—Interview with Riccardo Vescovo, published Jan. 17, 2006, in *Testata giornalistica dell'Università degli Studi di Palermo*; http://www.ateneonline-aol.it/060117ric.php.

6. "State of the World Population," UN Population Fund (UNFPA), 2000; http://www.unfpa.org/swp/2000/english/ch03.html.

7. Salman Masood, "Pakistan Tries to Curb 'Honor Killings,' " *New York Times*, Oct. 27, 2004; http://www.nytimes.com/2004/10/27/international/asia/27stan.html. Islam Online January 11 2007; http://www.islamonline.net/servlet/Satellite?c=Article_C&cid=1168265536796&pagename=Zone-English-News/NWELayout.

8. http://www.scci.org.pk/formerpre.htm.

9. Suzanne Goldberg, "A Question of Honour" *The Guardian,* May 27 1999; http://www.guardian.co.uk/world/1999/may/27/gender.uk1.

10. Amir H. Jafri, *Honour Killing: Dilemma, Ritual, Understanding* (Oxford: Oxford University Press, 2008): 67. *Ghairat* is used for honor in Urdu as well as in Pashto.

11. *Pakistan: Honour Killings of Girls and Women*, Amnesty International, September 1999 (AI Index: ASA 33/18/99). Kalpana Sharma, "Killing for Honour," *The Hindu,* Chennai, India, April 25, 1999, retrieved through Westlaw, June 6, 2009, Ref: 1999 WLNR 4528908.

12. *Pakistan: Honour Killings of Girls and Women*, 5–6.

13. Galpin, "Woman's 'Honour' Killing Draws Protest in Pakistan."

14. Jafri, *op. cit.*, 125.

15. Zaffer Abbas, "Pakistan Fails to Condemn 'Honour' Killings," BBC Online, Aug. 3, 1999; http://news.bbc.co.uk/2/hi/south_asia/410422.stm.

16. Irfan Husain, "Those Without Voices," *Dawn Online Edition,* Karachi, Pakistan, Sept. 6, 2008; http://www.dawn.com/weekly/mazdak/20080609.htm.

17. Rabia Ali, *The Dark Side of "Honour": Women Victims in Pakistan* (Shirkat Gah Women's Resource Centre, Lahore, 2001): 30.

18. "MoC consulting stakeholders on new ATTA," *The Business Recorder,* Nov. 19, 2009; http://www.brecorder.com/index.php?id=988220.

19. See the discussion of Pashtun social structure in Ali Wardak, "Jirga—Power and Traditional Conflict Resolution in Afghanistan," in John Strawson, ed., *Law After Ground Zero* (London: Glasshouse Press, 2002): 191–92, 196. On the Pashtunwali, he cites N. Newell and R. Newell, *The Struggle for Afghanistan* (London: Cornell University Press, 1981): 23.

20. Jafri, *op. cit.*, 76.

21. *Ibid.*, 7.

22. *Ibid.*, 66, 123.

23. http://www.paklinks.com/gs/culture-literature-linguistics/148820-ghairat.html.

24. Jason Bourke, "Teenage Rape Victim Executed for Bringing 'Shame' to Her Tribesmen" *The Guardian,* April 18, 1999; http://www.guardian.co.uk/Archive/Article/0,4273,3855659,00.html.

25. http://www.pakistani.org/pakistan/constitution/preamble.html.

26. *NCSW Report on the Qisas and Diyat Ordinance*, 68. I have not seen this claim reported elsewhere.

27. *Shamoon alias* v. *The State*, 1995 SCMR 1377, cited in *NCSW Report on Qisas and Diyat Ordinance*, 35.

28. In the case of slavery, too, legal emancipation is only the beginning. See Kwame Anthony Appiah, "What's Wrong with Slavery?" in Martin Bunzl and K. Anthony Appiah, eds. *Buying Freedom* (Princeton: Princeton University Press, 2007): 249–58.

29. Naeem Shakir, "Women and religious minorities under the Hudood Laws

in Pakistan," posted on July 2, 2004, at http://www.article2.org/mainfile.php/0303/144/.

30. David Montero, "Rape Law Reform Roils Pakistan's Islamists," *Christian Science Monitor*, Nov. 17, 2006; http://www.csmonitor.com/2006/1117/p07s02-wosc.html.

31. For examples, see Jafri, *op. cit.*, 115–16.

32. *State of Human Rights in 2008* (Lahore: Human Rights Commission of Pakistan, 2009): 134.

33. Beena Sarwar, "No 'Honour' in Killing," *News International*, Sept. 3, 2008; http://www.thenews.com.pk/daily_detail.asp?id=133499. (Beena Sarwar is not, so far as I know, related to Samia Sarwar.)

34. I know, of course, that when presented with a woman "taken in adultery," Christ says, "He that is without sin among you, let him first cast a stone at her" (John 8:7). But here, as elsewhere, Christ does not explicitly repudiate the laws of Moses; just as the Prophet Muhammad, in raising the required evidence for convictions of adultery, does not reject the traditional Arab view that stoning is the proper penalty.

35. See *Pakistan: Honour Killings of Girls and Women*, 8.

36. See Jafri, *op. cit.*, 115–17.

37. *Ibid.*, 92–93.

38. There is a chain of public women's refuges called *Dar ul-Amans* in Pakistan, of which the first was founded in Lahore many years ago, but they are widely reputed to be very unfriendly places. See Meera Jamal, "Hapless Women Call Darul Aman 'No Less Than Prison,' " *Dawn Internet Edition*, Aug. 13, 2007; http://www.dawn.com/2007/08/13/local1.htm.

39. Galpin, "Woman's 'Honour' Killing Draws Protest in Pakistan."

40. Philip D. Curtin, *The Atlantic Slave Trade: A Census* (Madison: University of Wisconsin Press, 1969): 136.

CHAPTER 5: LESSONS AND LEGACIES

1. Alexis de Tocqueville, *De la démocratie en Amérique*, 5th edn. (Paris: Pagnerre, 1848), Vol. 4: 152–53.

2. Immanuel Kant, *Groundwork of the Metaphysics of Morals,* Cambridge Texts in the History of Philosophy, ed. Mary Gregor (Cambridge: Cambridge University Press, 1997): 7.

3. *Ibid.*, 11.

4. I discuss some of this recent work in moral psychology in my book *Experiments in Ethics* (Cambridge, MA: Harvard University Press, 2008).

5. John Locke, *The Works of John Locke in Nine Volumes,* 12th edn. (London: Rivington, 1824), Vol. 8, Chapter: Some Thoughts Concerning Education; http://oll.libertyfund.org/title/1444/81467/1930382.

6. Horace, *Sermones,* I, 6, ll. 7–8.

7. *Ibid.*, ll. 34–37.

8. Ascriptive identities to which one is assigned by birth, such as family membership, can, I should insist, be relevant bases for partiality. You are entitled (indeed, sometimes required) to treat A better than B solely because A is your sister and B is unrelated to you. But recognizing something as a form of partiality is recognizing that there is nothing intrinsically superior about those to whom one is partial: if there were, one's reasons for favoring them could be impartial. See Appiah, *The Ethics of Identity,* chapter 6.

9. David Hume, *Enquiries Concerning the Human Understanding and Concerning the Principles of Morals by David Hume,* ed. L. A. Selby-Bigge, M.A. 2nd edn. (Oxford: Clarendon Press, 1902), 265.

10. Newman, *The Idea of a University,* 208–11.

11. Rupert Brooke, "The Dead," from *1914: Five Sonnets* (London: Sidgwick & Jackson, 1914): 3.

12. For reasons for thinking this, see Paul Robinson, *Military Honour and Conduct of War: From Ancient Greece to Iraq* (London: Routledge, 2006).

13. Brennan and Pettit, *op. cit.,* 260.

14. This is the reverse of a public good: a public evil.

15. Atul Gawande, "The Cost Conundrum: What a Texas Town Can Teach Us About Health Care," *The New Yorker,* June 1, 2009; http://www.new yorker.com/reporting/2009/06/01/090601fa_fact_gawande.

16. "Rumsfeld Testifies Before Armed Services Committee," Transcript of Senate testimony on Friday, May 7, 2004, at washingtonpost.com, http://www.washingtonpost.com/wp-dyn/articles/A8575-2004May7.html.

17. Ian Fishback, letter to Senator John McCain, printed in *The Washington Post*, September 28, 2005, under the headline "A Matter of Honor"; http://www.washingtonpost.com/wp-dyn/content/article/2005/09/27/AR2005092701527_pf.html. See also Tara McKelvey, *Monstering: Inside America's Policy of Secret Interrogations and Torture in the Terror War* (New York: Basic Books, 2008): 6–7.

18. Coleen Rowley, "Ian Fishback," *Time* magazine, Apr. 30, 2006; http://www.time.com/time/magazine/article/0,9171,1187384,00.html.

19. McKelvey, *op. cit.* 179.

20. Tim Dickinson, "The Solider: Capt. Ian Fishback," *Rolling Stone*, Dec. 15, 2005; http://www.rollingstone.com/news/story/8957325/capt_ian_fishback.

21. McKelvey, *op. cit.*, 179.

22. Nicholas Kristof, Foreword to Mukhtar Mai's *In the Name of Honor: A Memoir*, xiv–xv.

INDEX

Page numbers beginning with 227 refer to notes.

ABOUT THE AUTHOR

Kwame Anthony Appiah is the Laurance S. Rockefeller University Professor of Philosophy and the University Center for Human Values at Princeton University. He is currently president of the PEN American Center, which supports international literary fellowship and free expression alongside the more than 140 other PEN Centers around the world. He is also a member of the American Academy of Arts and Letters.